CAN I
SAY
THAT?

CAN I SAY THAT?

HOW UNSAFE QUESTIONS LEAD US TO THE REAL GOD

BRENNA BLAIN

W PUBLISHING GROUP

AN IMPRINT OF THOMAS NELSON

Can I Say That?

Published in Nashville, Tennessee, by W Publishing, an imprint of Thomas Nelson.

Thomas Nelson titles may be purchased in bulk for educational, business, fundraising, or sales promotional use. For information, please email SpecialMarkets@ThomasNelson.com.

Published in association with Alive Literary Agency, www.aliveliterary.com.

Unless otherwise noted, Scripture quotations are taken from the Holy Bible, New International Version®, NIV®. Copyright © 1973, 1978, 1984, 2011 by Biblica, Inc.® Used by permission of Zondervan. All rights reserved worldwide. www.zondervan.com. The "NIV" and "New International Version" are trademarks registered in the United States Patent and Trademark Office by Biblica, Inc.®

Scripture quotations marked NLT are from Holy Bible, New Living Translation. © 1996, 2004, 2015 by Tyndale House Foundation. Used by permission of Tyndale House Ministries, Carol Stream, Illinois, 60188. All rights reserved.

This book is written as a source of information only. The information contained in this book should not be considered a substitute for the advice, decisions, or judgment of the reader's physician or other professional advisor.

Some personal names and identifying details have been changed to protect the privacy of the individuals involved.

Any internet addresses, phone numbers, or company or product information printed in this book are offered as a resource and are not intended in any way to be or to imply an endorsement by Thomas Nelson, nor does Thomas Nelson vouch for the existence, content, or services of these sites, phone numbers, companies, or products beyond the life of this book.

ISBN 978-1-4003-3996-9 (audiobook)
ISBN 978-1-4003-3995-2 (ePub)
ISBN 978-1-4003-3994-5 (softcover)

Library of Congress Control Number: 2024933164

Printed in the United States of America
24 25 26 27 28 LBC 5 4 3 2 1

To my dad, for the relentless encouragement
and for choosing redemption. I love you.

TRIGGER WARNING

This book includes sensitive material related to the author's experiences with

- sexual abuse (chapters 1, 2, 7, 8, 10),
- same-sex attraction (chapters 1, 2),
- depression and other mental health issues (chapter 4),
- an eating disorder (chapters 9, 10),
- suicide attempts (chapter 4),
- spiritual abuse (chapters 3, 4), and
- a miscarriage (chapter 10).

References to these issues appear throughout the book but especially in the areas listed above. I invite you to be mindful of your own sensitivities and how you can give yourself care and kindness as you read.

CONTENTS

FOREWORD

Brenna has quickly become one of my favorite younger voices in the church today. That's because Brenna is raw, uncut, honest, and utterly addicted to the gospel. Not that fluffy, pie-in-the-sky, plastic gospel that you might see plastered over so many church-going faces today. Brenna's gospel is the real thing. It's about a Savior who delights in really messed up people; a Savior who promises us suffering and hardship, not endless comfort in a padded world. Brenna's gospel—it's not Brenna's but Jesus', of course—is the good news that God sent His Son to enter into our pain, experience our humanity, and deal with our suffering by His own suffering, bidding us to follow Him in this complex journey of life filled with joy and doubt, grief and victory.

Brenna has been through a lot. More than most people endure over a lifetime. She speaks not from some kind of idealized view of the world, since she hasn't seen such a world. Her story is also not one where all her trials and sin and suffering are things of the past, as she waltzes through a garden of roses on the other side of victory. Just when you think Brenna has arrived (happily married, no more depression, white picket fence), she ends up in a psych ward. Brenna speaks from a place where most of us are currently living—the real world—a place where things don't always seem to work out, where depression and anxiety and suicidal thoughts accompany our daily devotions.

Yes, God is good. God is near to us. And God protects us and loves us and cares for us. But, for whatever reason, fathers still sexually assault their children; mothers abandon their kids; good people are addicted to porn; and believers in Christ are victims of genocide—sometimes by the hands of fellow Christians. And on and on it goes. This world is filled with evil, and sometimes it's very difficult to believe that God is good.

But He is good. It's one thing for some theologian to tell you that and to quote all the verses at you that say God is good. It's quite another for someone like Brenna, who has experienced—and continues to experience—depression, unwanted same-sex attraction, tendencies to self-harm, and ongoing suicidal thoughts—to say, with all honesty and with an earthy passion: God is good!

I truly believe that Brenna's story as told in this book is the way of the future for evangelical Christianity. Everyone is tired of short answers to thick questions, of assuming that Christianity is nice and easy. What the evangelical church needs is more honesty, more humility, more lament alongside our long bouts of celebration. And Brenna gives us a model of what this looks like.

The genius of this book is that Brenna creates space for us to ask hard questions and be okay if we don't receive simple answers—or no answers at all. In the midst of our doubts and questions and fears and hopes, Brenna reminds us that God is good. He is present with us not just in spite of our pain, but also because of our pain. After all, the God who revealed Himself to us in His crucified Son knows very well what it is to experience pain and suffering.

—*Preston Sprinkle*
Bestselling author and host of the
Theology in the Raw podcast

PART 1

SITTING IN DISCOMFORT

CHAPTER 1

IS FAITH WORTH PRESERVING?

Take off your coat and stay awhile!"

It was a Tuesday night, and I was at one of our regular practice sessions at the band leader's home. I was there with two other middle schoolers to practice the worship songs we'd play the next week. My bass guitar was heavy, and I was feeling lightheaded and sweating buckets. Fearing I might black out, I quietly asked for a chair.

But I wouldn't take off my coat.

If you saw me in sixth grade, the likelihood of you seeing me without a coat on was astronomically low. No matter the temperature, I clung to my coat for dear life. Maybe you're reading this and you already know why, because you wore a coat forever ago too, or because you're wearing one now. But if you don't know, it's okay. I didn't know why for a long time either.

The summer after my freshman year of high school, I got a

job as a camp counselor. Since I was going to be working with children, I was required to read a "signs of abuse" packet. I remember getting to the sexual and physical abuse section and preparing my heart for such a heavy topic.

I started reading. And I stopped breathing.

I read more and more and more. Almost every sign of abuse I read about—spending unusual amounts of time alone, avoiding the removal of clothing, experiencing changes to mood and personality and self-image, losing interest in friendships and activities, self-harm—were signs I exhibited in my own life. Every single one. I sat there in shock.

Then, like a nightmare, I recalled a night at basketball practice when I was ten. I genuinely thought because of my height and ability I would go on to play college ball, maybe even go to the WNBA. Granted, I was young, and this was just community basketball, but I loved this sport and took it seriously. This season felt especially important as it would be one of my only distractions from my home life. There, pain was fresh and discomfort evident as my grandma had recently died from cancer and my parents were newly separated.

But playing a game wasn't the distraction I received.

After practice that night, I climbed into the car, reeling inside, and sobbed. My mom tried to figure out what had happened to me, but I couldn't name it. I felt so much shame and confusion and fear. The only thing I could name was my discontentment. I insisted that I had to quit, trying to convince her that I no longer loved basketball.

This, of course, didn't make sense, and quitting wasn't something my parents would let me do, but I was persistent. I could not go back. Somehow, I managed to talk my mom into letting me forgo the rest of the season without any real explanation.

From then on, I kept my coat on everywhere I went. The extra layers protected me and helped me walk into strange places without debilitating anxiety. They hid my body, which I viewed with distorted and unkind eyes and later would even abuse. Although I eventually shed that outer layer of physical protection, a different, more complex layer of protection started to form around me: my personality and my beliefs.

I'd sit on a metal chair in our church's youth room, alone or beside a leader who was just trying to be nice to me. I'd sit through sermons about lying or being mean or disrespecting my parents. All those lessons may be valid and important, but at the time, they fed my soul a lie I'm sure Satan took delight in: *My reality doesn't matter, and God doesn't care.* I'd sigh to myself as these words would replay in my mind while I walked out of youth group. Sure, like every middle school kid, I struggled with kindness, and I didn't always respect my parents. But I'd also been molested.

All those years ago, in a gym, my ten-year-old self walked into basketball practice with her innocence intact, and she walked out trying to gather and hold together all the shattered pieces of herself. This was a brokenness I never heard anyone mention from the pulpit or with a Bible in their hands.

My entire upbringing involved church and Sunday school, youth camps and Bible studies. I was told over and over and over again, "God is good! He is our comfort and our joy, and He is with us in our hardship."

Well, I thought, *He must be all those things unless that hardship includes abuse, or parental separation, or addiction.*

My reality was incongruent with the gospel people were teaching me. God was good, unless you had been abused—then, there wasn't much He could do for you. God was near, unless you felt emotionally alone. God was our comfort, unless the comfort you needed was due to something too uncomfortable to talk about.

A god who cared about lying but not my wounding wasn't a god at all, but a tyrant. I didn't want to be told he loved me. The God of the Christian church apparently wasn't big or caring enough for my problems.

So I made a choice: I would continue faking my way through church as long as I lived at home to appease my Christian parents. Once I was old enough to make the choice, however, I'd walk away from this "empty" religion. False hope was more depressing to me than searching for something real, even if I never found it.

But I just couldn't quiet Him.

The Whisper and the Shout

Often I'd be practicing guitar, avoiding homework, or spending time with friends, when my wounded ten-year-old self would enter my mind, bowl cut and all. I'd wonder, *Does God even care?* Something inside me would whisper back, *I think He does. I don't know how, but I think He does.*

It became my habit to sit for a very long time, doing nothing but contemplating that whisper: *I think He does.* A memory often accompanied those words—another voice, yelling. It was a man wearing a black hoodie and a baseball cap. His ears were gauged, his nose pierced, his arms tattooed. He was nothing like any of the pastors I knew, but his appearance felt oddly inviting to me.

He was the middle school pastor at Legacy Park Church.

When he yelled, you could really hear it. His voice reverberated out of two mounted speakers and straight into my chest.

"Some of you think no one knows that you struggle with porn, but it's stealing from you!" the pastor shouted as he paced on the unsteady portable stage. The entire room was silent, shocked, squirming. I, too, was shocked by his words—not because they felt taboo, but because in them, I felt recognized.

In that church gym, the vibrations of sound no longer felt physical, but emotional and spiritual. As adolescents, we were being addressed as humans who experienced real, deep, personal issues. A subject like porn had never come up in my other churches or youth groups, but now an adult—a pastor—was acknowledging that even people our age could have struggles and secret sins. Porn wasn't a personal struggle of mine, and if I told you I remembered the rest of the sermon, I'd be lying. So why did God keep bringing this memory to mind as I wrestled with my doubts?

Perhaps those words held something beyond a recognition of our sin. Perhaps they spoke more deeply by answering the question I was asking underneath.

God cared about my faith.

God cared about my abuse.

God cared about my human condition.

God cared.

Right . . . ?

Brick by Brick

What I know now—and what I wish I'd known then—is that suffering is universal. It's shared, spread, and reaped. Through generations of families, communities, and countries, there is not one person who remains untouched by the plight of sin. (Thanks, Adam and Eve.) So maybe you have asked the same questions I've asked. You've wondered how Christians could call their God good. The church doesn't feel safe. Or you're just trying to help guide another questioner in your life toward what you've come to know to be true.

You are not alone. While questions and doubts are the natural outflow of the brokenness we all experience in the world, the process of voicing them can feel awfully lonely. As time goes on, the questions don't fade. In fact, if left unaddressed, they begin to stack up. We all collect these questions, like bricks in a bag.

You might look around and wonder why your bag weighs heavily on your shoulders while others seem to have no bricks at all. I promise you this is not the case. Some might hide the weight well, afraid that they are the only ones who consider questions that seem unmentionable in Christian spaces. With fear of condemnation or anxiety from past rejection, they hide the fact that these bricks weigh on their hearts and minds, never giving voice to the questions that burden them.

I am telling you now, this is not the road for you.

But if everyone has bricks, if everyone carries the load of unrelenting questions, what other option is there?

Some hide the weight. And others have found a place to relinquish their bricks, those weighty questions and beliefs. Rather than tossing them away or getting rid of them, they position and layer them intentionally. They hold their bricks, weighing them, wondering whether they want to add each one to their foundation. They ask, "Is this brick, this belief, one on which I can build my life and faith?"

CAN I SAY THAT?

Sometimes those beliefs feel like rubble or sand—riddled with doubt and not sturdy enough to support a house. But even that gravel, that sand, has a critical role in the construction of a building. So out of these bricks they have built homes where they dwell, fireplaces where they sit, and kitchens where they gather. Their bricks are not forgotten or dismissed but incorporated, remembered, and seen. They have a purpose.

We all have questions and doubts that hold great significance, but they don't need to weigh us down. In fact, when stewarded well, they can become foundational to our living. They can lead us to powerful truths to count on. I'd say I've become someone who inhabits a space built by questions, and I know many others who are the same way.

Not one of us constructed our foundation on our own. We leaned on someone else who came near and looked closely at our bricks, considered their size, shape, and origins, and helped us place them with gentleness and precision where they would serve the entire structure. All this takes work, takes time, takes a miracle. And it is not wishful thinking.

It is the process I want you to join me on.

This process requires honesty—that is a given. We have to understand the materials we're producing in order to best implement it as corners, walls, and staircases. But you won't be doing it alone. In fact, what if I go first?

My story isn't tidy. At times it lacks grace and reeks of anger. It's overflowing with brokenness and colored by grief. Even now as I write, I still struggle. I'll share some about my mental health diagnoses, sexuality, abuse, and eating disorder. All the monumental screeches of the brakes on my faith journey. The parts some people wish I would not bring up.

Maybe you can relate. And maybe, as you keep turning the pages, you will feel safe enough to be honest—maybe more honest than you have ever been—about your own story, hurts, fears, questions, and doubts.

There is something else you should know before we step forward together.

I am on this road with you as a fellow wanderer. I may have been here a little longer and gained a sense of the terrain. I have a compass, some worn boots, and an eagerness to climb. But I didn't create this road or the neatly layered bricks currently under construction in my life. Those have come about by that someone else. That Miracle Worker. The Architect.

Into Wild Spaces

You might flinch at those descriptions of God, I know. What if you don't believe He exists, that He really is a miracle worker? What if you are hoping to catch a break from Him? You might be tired of looking up and crying, "Are You even there? Do You even see me?"

But before you decide this isn't the type of road you want to be on, can I tell you something?

Sometimes we have to change what we're doing to experience something new. It's like looking up at a few stars, searching the airspace to pick out a constellation or two. You might not see the Milky Way, though—millions of stars spilled out against the sky. The city lights pollute your view; you have to get away from the familiar spaces if you want to see a million dazzling stars spread across the heavens. Out beyond the polluted spaces, the wilderness has something more. It has always existed, but we have not always had an unobstructed view. Will you come with me to see it, from a different perspective?

I can't promise it will be easy. I don't know what you will experience along our trek into the wild. In some places we might have similar muscle aches or hunger pains, but in others, God may show you constellations I have never seen before. There may be experiences that will seem profound to me and ordinary to you.

No matter the case, consider this book a guide, that it might help you choose to take this first step. I am not sure what is around the corner, but I do know the direction we are headed.

We'll spend time with questions that too often function as an off-ramp from Christianity. The ones that bring destruction or are never voiced inside the walls or circles of Christianity. The ones that haven't been readily addressed by churches or uttered behind pulpits but hold a lot of space in our minds. We will ask them out loud, together. We will give them voice.

We'll take a close look at some nice churchy words, the ones we roll our eyes at or assume we've exhausted the meaning of. *Bible. Pray. Sin. Love.* This time, though, we will assume the role of surgeon. With intention and care, we will cut into the layers of these seemingly ordinary practices and ideas. And as we scrape away the cancer induced by the brokenness of this world, we will uncover their original design and function, which might be more startling and countercultural than we'd expect.

We'll also explore why all this matters in our real lives. The mess of relationships and community, the reality of pain, and the dullness of the in-between that interrupt any kind of lofty thoughts about God. We can hold truth in our head, but to live out that truth, to embody the faith that exists in our brain, is no small feat. And yet, people live inside humble walls made from those heavy bricks, and they hold together pain and hard relationships and mundane days—all while embodying a quiet joy. We'll see how they do it.

And in the end we will ask the first question again. *Is faith worth preserving*? Maybe your answer right now is a merited "hell no" and you wonder if the time it will take to digest these words is even worth it. That is a fair question. Maybe it can be an exercise in debating a view you really won't agree with, or one in empathy for the "other." You don't and probably won't end up siding with me on every single conclusion. But I'd like to focus on what we have in common.

You and I can walk this trek together because we no longer care to assimilate to the legalistic culture of faith we have witnessed around us. We will not hold our tongues for fear of rocking the boat.

But let's not run away either.

What will running away do? And what good could come from discarding our bricks when there might be a blueprint for them? Many churches might not want our questions, but choosing to leave leaves them minus one image bearer. It does not teach the church to wrestle with or ask the questions out loud.

But resistance can be peacefully disruptive. Choosing to stand, feet planted, questioning God out loud in the very circles that taught us His name, will shake the atmosphere. It dares to say, "Show us Your character." For those who witness the question, it leaves them at risk of witnessing the answer.

And if Jesus is who He says He is, those answers are peacefully disruptive. Shockingly good. Undeniably real. Might we questioners be in these circles for a purpose?

Are you ready?

Me neither. In fact, this book, these words, are the most vulnerable thing I have ever done, but we can take one step at a time, together.

Let's be curious and honest.

Let's not hold back or jump to conclusions.

Let's use this space to be our real selves and sit with our stories, to say where we are and what's not making sense, to wrestle and question.

Where will all our openness and wondering take us?

If it's anything like where I've been on this journey so far, every moment will be worth it.

CHAPTER 2

AM I SAFE HERE?

My face burned when I read the words on the screen. Here it was, my secret now existing in someone else's mind. All I ever wanted was to be known, but not like this and not this part of me. I wanted to feel seen and accepted in a clean, simple way, not have a spotlight thrown on my messy human complexities. Every muscle in my body tensed, screaming, "Don't let us be seen!" My body knew my shame well, and it writhed to see someone else knowing it too.

"Are you gay?"

I readjusted my seat in front of the family computer, holding back tears and looking around to see if anyone was close by. I searched for a desperate excuse as to why my blog, with my name and picture clearly attached to it, was littered with images of girls holding hands and cuddling, which weren't supposed to be associated with someone who went to church. But no excuse could make sense of those photos other than what was true: I liked girls.

And I hated the idea of anyone knowing that.

I had learned years before that certain people were incompatible with Christianity. When I was young, I thought it was people who wore thong bathing suits or did drugs. As I got older and I listened to the irate, outspoken people at Westboro Baptist Church, I gathered that gay people were making God angriest, since He was sending them natural disasters and wars. With no real counterarguments or nuanced conversations taking place in my circles of faith, this felt like truth.

Questions churned in my head, questions maybe you've asked before too: *Am I too tainted for the church, the house of God? If I ever confessed to my struggles within the walls of a church, would I be safe there?*

And I couldn't escape the haunting statement that reverberated in my mind: *God hates gay people.*

The notion of God hating anyone was confusing when I was seven. Most of the narratives I knew about God were ones of love, not hate. It felt sad when I was nine, when I started to learn about my own willful disobedience and sinful condition. When I was ten, it started to make sense. If God could let me be molested, He might as well hate entire groups of people too. A God who didn't care about abuse could also be an abuser.

But it was adolescent me who really had to grapple with the weight of this idea. Because this Brenna, who previously lacked the words to express her abuse or voice her doubts, knew her attractions had a name, one that burst from the loudest of mouths, boiling out of them in hate. As I came to believe them—that God hated gay people—a huge ditch formed between God and me.

What do you do when the center of your entire existence suddenly wants nothing to do with you?

You beg Him to make you into something acceptable, something without struggle.

And if you're like adolescent me, you pray to be made straight.

Attraction and Torture

I must have been twelve when I recognized a difference between me and my female peers. Their mouths and brains and binders became occupied with the allure of musicians and movie stars who all had one thing in common: they were men. I, on the other hand, seemed to be bewitched by . . . not men. And that's when the contortion started.

During the first week of seventh grade, I stared intently at pictures of celebrities cut out of magazines and glued to my friends' notebooks—a man with long, orange hair; a man with tattoos; a man with brown hair and messy clothes. I studied them hard so I could know how to make my binder match theirs.

Still, without names and with my disinterest in popular male figures, I knew I was bound to have a collage of "stereotypical young men" stock photos, so I invited a friend over to help. Sidney was edgy. She wore skinny jeans before anyone else did and had dyed black hair. I didn't know anyone who didn't like her because, on top of being fully herself, she was also significantly kind. We printed out some pictures of Christian bands like Family Force 5 and Underoath, but, unsurprisingly, I wasn't completely satisfied with my binder.

"I . . . I wish I could put, like, a girl on here. But that's weird, right?"

Before I could even finish my sentence, Sidney was loudly

objecting. "Why couldn't you put a girl?!" Soon she was Googling Kat Von D, who we both had an affinity for, and Kat joined the group of guys on my binder.

The next day at school, I pulled out my no-longer-plain notebook with great pride. My desk partner leaned in eagerly to look, excited to see some "hot boys." I flashed a smile at Sidney, feeling some sense of relief that I could be a little bit more of myself outwardly—that is until I heard: "You put a girl . . . on your notebook? Isn't that like . . . gay?"

Have you ever jumped into water that was much colder than you anticipated? The shock freezes your body and takes the breath right out of your lungs. Your body is sitting with one reality—*I am dying*—while your mind is holding another—*I need to survive.* That is how hearing *gay* for the first time felt. Everyone at my school knew I went to church. Everyone at my school, from what I knew, was straight. And everyone at my school might as well have been staring daggers at me.

Before I even had time to form a single word, much less a reply, Sidney butted in. "That's not gay . . . she can have cool humans on her notebook."

If Sidney said it, almost everyone took it to heart.

But even once people's eyes were no longer on me, that experience formed one of the heaviest bricks I ever tried to carry alone. With its sharp edges and cold weight, it cut deep into my skin. I now had an open wound that reminded me every single day: *You cannot let this part of you be known. No one wants to know this kind of dirty. If it's found out, you will not be safe. You will be a social pariah.*

Who of us hasn't felt some version of this?

Maybe I'm not gay, I told myself countless times. If a boy paid attention to me, I said it. When I saw picket signs with fire and pejorative terms, I said it with fear. And at night, when I'd sink underneath my pink comforter, eyes welled up with tears after a day of my heart beating in my throat from noticing a pair of big brown eyes, I'd say it with a pocketknife pressed into my wrist. When wishful thinking failed, torture and prayer seemed to be the only options left. These would become habits that would stick with me for years.

Lord, if You're real, would You just make me straight?

Now might be a good time to remind you that this book is not all about sexuality or my journey with that specifically. It is about asking our hardest, deepest questions, and, for a while, my question was about sexuality.

Maybe yours is something like, *Would You just lead that person to like me? Would You just free me from this addiction? Would You bring peace to my family? Would You keep me from constantly screwing up?*

If I had written out my version of this plea every time I prayed it, my walls would have become pitch black with ink. Every night. Every single night for what felt like years, I begged the God who didn't really care for me to make some way for me to be able to experience the goodness of forever with Him.

And you know what changed? Nothing. My prayers became more desperate and my arms more scarred as my attractions continually brought me right back to the same place. I'd scream at my heart every time it beat in the presence of another woman who left me enraptured against my will.

What is left for you when that is your reality? When you never once asked to hold feelings for someone you're not supposed to have, yet the attraction is a force like gravity? No matter what you do, you cannot change this aspect of your existence. You've prayed your voice hoarse, cut your arms raw, and nothing has changed. You no longer can deny that your bed is made at the gates of hell.

Maybe you do what I did: Lie in that bed. Lean into the gravity.

As my prayers tapered off, I began to stoke my longings. If hell was inevitable, I figured I might as well run toward the only happiness I would know during my lifetime. I met other gay teens online and asked the ones who were already out how their parents received them and how they knew it was time to share publicly—all the questions that held great anxiety for me.

At age fourteen, I shared my secret with my closest friends, none of whom treated me differently, despite their different reactions—from "As long as you're happy, I'm happy" to "You know this means you're going to hell, right?"

I caught a glimpse of what it would look like to come out to the secular world, and it was inviting. That world didn't view me as gross. It loved what I loved. It fed my desires. It didn't ask me to change. It invited me to indulge. I binged movies and TV shows with lesbian couples and I dreamed about the day I would be loved by someone I was wildly in love with.

And it was still all under wraps.

Because I went to church.

It Didn't Make Sense

After sitting in church for years hearing that God wanted me to obey my parents and sensing that He could offer only deafening silence about my abuse, I concluded that church wasn't the place for me. I hated it. But being conflict avoidant and eager for friends, I didn't fight my parents' request that I attend.

"You don't have to go to our church, but we do ask that you'd go to a church while you're living at home."

My childhood best friend, Mary, also had recently escaped the dreaded Baptist church. After she spent time at Legacy Park Church over a summer when I was away, she gave me a call.

"I think you'd really like Emerson—she'd be our small-group leader. Everyone's chill. I'll be there tonight if you want to come."

Mary had a social ease that I lacked; she could have a normal conversation with almost anyone. Me? I had a mullet. A mullet that had previously been a black-and-bleached shadow box, so I looked like a skunk. A depressed skunk . . . who was secretly gay . . . walks into a church. There's no punch line. Anyway, while I loved Mary, I did not think a youth group she enjoyed would be something I'd enjoy. But I gave it a shot anyway.

A lump grew in my throat as I climbed out of our van and walked toward the massive group of teens. My eyes scanned the crowd for Mary, but before I could find her, someone stopped me.

"Hi, I'm Jon, the youth pastor here! What's your name and where do you go to school?"

I hated awkward introductions like this. With minimal eye contact, I answered his questions and trailed off as soon as I spotted Mary. It wouldn't matter anyway; I probably wouldn't come back. Even if I did, no one would want to know me here—I mean, really know me.

But Mary was right: I loved Emerson. In fact, I loved just about everyone. After spending years at a different church hopelessly trying to make friends, I visited this youth group once and left with an invitation to be a part of a small group.

My interest in the small group itself was lower than low, but I couldn't deny wanting to see if I could possibly fit in here. Week two came, and I jumped out of the van and searched for Mary again.

"Hey, Brenna! It's great to see you again!" Jon said, grinning.

The singular look I gave him in response had to have been borderline insulting. *Why must this man always pop out of nowhere to try to talk to me when I am just trying to blend in and find my friends?!* I grumbled to myself. *I don't do friendly, I don't do small talk, and I certainly don't have any interest in knowing adult dudes who think God is worth knowing.*

"Uh, yep," I replied and gave a closed-mouth fake smile as my eyes continued to search. Then Emerson ran up to me, genuinely excited I had come back.

That night I met even more kids—kids who were in bands, kids who listened to 94.7, the alternative Portland radio station I liked, kids who actually thought my hair was cool. It didn't take long for me to fall in love with these people. Sure, I didn't care for what church was about, but that didn't matter in the face of *belonging.*

If I skipped a night, someone texted me to say they missed me. I got invited to birthday parties and game nights. And every Wednesday I found myself looking forward, with real excitement, to youth group—which we called Refuge.

I know. It didn't make sense. Fourteen-year-old me hated church, was afraid of God, and was absolutely, undeniably gay.

These things don't make you a good candidate to be a youth group kid. They make you depressed. But, as long as I kept my secret a secret, *I belonged*. And that was everything for me.

Refuge

A year later at age fifteen, if you asked me who my closest friends were, I would have named that entire small group. We spent weekends and evenings together, and Wednesdays were the highlight of my week. Why? Because people liked me for me. Well, most of me—the parts I would allow them to see. While my secret was still intact, my longings persisted, and I became careless about covering them up.

And when you don't take care, you get found out.

I can't tell you what day it was. I know it was fall and I know I almost threw up. My Tumblr page (an online blog) was private; I thought I had a pretty good read on who would and wouldn't care about the contents. Besides, if anyone was going to say something, they would say it right away, wouldn't they? They would talk to me first, right?

That didn't happen.

Like a crime scene, every piece of my hidden soul was collected and sent to Emerson, my small-group leader. With evidence in hand, she asked the question we both already knew the answer to.

"Are you gay?"

That was the moment that left my face burning and my vision blurring as I sat in front of the family computer. Stepping away from the screen was only a temporary defense. Emerson and I had plans to get coffee that weekend, and I didn't drive yet, so even if I canceled, I knew she'd still show up to get me.

And when that moment arrived, my ears burned again as I climbed into her car, barely breathing. *God, I know I don't talk to you often, but if you could just let us be hit by another car, that would be great*, I prayed, sinking further into the passenger seat. I loved Emerson, but I hated this.

We walked silently into the coffee shop, which I was paranoid was full of Christian Republicans. My entire body at this point had to be bright red, and as I searched for the courage to bolt out the front door, Emerson spit out the first set of words.

"Brenna, what is going on? Do you like girls?"

I stared at Emerson and searched for the only lie that would make sense.

"I mean, I'm a Christian, so I'm not going to, like, do anything about it. I mostly like guys anyway."

I never was good at lying. Except maybe to myself. I thought she bought it and that was the end of that. I'd be more careful online; I'd go to youth group until I graduated college. Then I'd just stop going to church. It was a really good plan, until it wasn't.

The next week before youth group, Emerson texted me, "Hey girl, I am not really sure what to do, so I had to tell Jon."

You might as well have shot me in the heart.

Our youth group was the place I felt most like my true self—where I felt genuinely happy; it was the only thing I looked forward to in life. Now it felt like the furthest thing from that. To tell a teen that their pastor from their traditional church found out they are gay might as well be a death sentence. (I am not exaggerating; look at the statistics. "One study of LGBTQ young adults ages 18–24 found that parents' religious beliefs about homosexuality were associated with double the risk of attempting suicide in the past year" (Gibbs & Goldbach, 2015[1]). Add to the fact that I was already suicidal, and you start to understand what exactly this meant for me.

I figured Emerson would be chill enough not to tell my parents or freak out. But Jon? I didn't know him. In fact, the only interactions with Jon that stood out to me were: (1) for some reason he remembered my name, and (2) at one point he'd called my parents as a mandatory reporter after I'd told Emerson I'd been self-harming. So, to me, Jon had a good memory and was a giant snitch. Awesome qualities for this situation.

I had a choice to make. *Do I quit going to youth group and subsequently quit seeing my friends? Or do I face possibly the worst interaction I could ever have with a pastor in my life? Do I ditch the one thing that has made me feel some sense of joy over the last year? Or do I risk a terrible conversation, my parents finding out, and probably getting asked to leave the church? Will this information follow me the rest of my life? Will I be forced out of the closet? What will the other leaders think—the other Christians in my life?*

Was I safe?

Not Just Me, but Us

Many of us have felt this kind of anxiety. Maybe for you it hasn't been about sexuality; maybe it's been a looming divorce or a

---

1. Research@thetrevorproject.org. "Religiosity and Suicidality Among LGBTQ Youth." The Trevor Project, April 14, 2020. https://www.thetrevorproject.org /research-briefs/religiosity-and-suicidality-among-lgbtq-youth/.

dependence on alcohol. Maybe no one knows you're transgender or that you've been abused by a member of the church staff. Maybe you've had an abortion or you're chronically suicidal. Maybe you're a sex worker or you sell drugs. Maybe you watch a lot of porn or you starve yourself. Maybe you've hurt a lot of people or you're hiding from someone who has hurt you.

Whatever it is, when you think about it coming to light in the presence of Christian people, you feel like you would rather die. You feel like throwing up or running away. Because at the core of it, you feel unsafe.

And there's plenty of good reasons for feeling threatened. You and I have seen the hatred, the pain, and the lack of safety thrown onto those who have been honest in Christian circles. There have been countless "Westboros" across the world at any given time. They've stood between you and clinics. They've screamed profanities while clutching Bibles to their chests. They've told you to be quiet for the sake of unity or demanded confession for the sake of salvation. They've made church a social club where you have to be "this clean to get in," all while the person who "made you dirty" is leading the entire thing. And when you've pressed in a little harder or stood on your tiptoes just to try and get a glimpse of this Jesus person they so adamantly need to protect, they deem you incompatible.

You're left with two options.

You can comply, blend in, stay quiet, and never dare to ask *those questions* or share your entire self.

Or you can simply leave. Maybe you look for a different Jesus on the way out, or maybe you just throw it all out the window.

Let me tell you about what happened when I leaned hard into option one.

Can I Talk to You?

Fifteen-year-old me imagined every scenario of what might happen if I went back to youth group. I eventually concluded that I could go and simply avoid Jon. More than a hundred kids showed up on any given night, so it was possible to avoid someone. If they ended up heading your direction, all you had to do was squat and walk fast the other way (I am speaking from experience). With this false confidence I decided to go back to youth group, believing I'd be safe as long as I remained hidden.

This did not happen.

After surviving twenty-five minutes of (the absolute worst) free time mingling in the lobby, we all walked into the sanctuary for a game. Within only one minute I saw Jon, and like the shock of unexpected pain, his kind eyes caught mine. I should have ran or moved or just ignored him as he walked toward me, but I couldn't think fast enough.

"Hey, Brenna, can I talk to you later?" he asked.

For the rest of the night, I felt as if a bomb had gone off. I couldn't hear or see anything clearly; my ears rang and my heart pounded throughout every inch of my body. I don't know how I managed to sit quietly without puking or blacking out. I wanted the service to be over so I could escape, but I also wanted it to never end so I wouldn't have to talk with Jon. I'd never experienced such an overwhelming fight-or-flight response in my fifteen years of life.

Have you ever been confronted by someone who hated you? By someone who took great issue with you or publicly embodied the complete opposite of who you are? You prepare yourself for a yelling match, a communal shaming, a physical altercation, or a

27

great wave of tears and embarrassment. Your blood pressure sky-rockets as your entire being is consumed with one thought: *What happens next?* You feel this way because, whether emotionally, spiritually, or physically, you sense that you are unsafe.

After the service, it was time to break into small groups. As I headed toward our designated meeting area, Jon approached me and quietly said, "Hey, let's go over there and sit down," pointing to some chairs toward the back corner of the sanctuary.

I shuffled my feet as if they were made of lead. No matter how much I wanted to avoid it, the moment had come. I was about to lose the only thing I loved at that point in life. I sat, hands shaking, eyes already watering. Jon smiled a closed-mouth smile, and I braced myself for facing such an unsafe moment.

It was the same unsafe feeling I'd had hearing chanting about how much God hated gay people, or seeing signs vehemently rejecting them, or feeling the rage of protestors at pride parades. It felt, to me, like the kind of high-risk, terrifying atmosphere that causes so many to hide and never be seen, or run a distance our legs should never even know.

I stuck my chin out, ready for the precarious space to do what it had always done: assault, damage, and wound. I closed my eyes and got ready for impact.

I did not know that I was about to experience an embodiment of Christ so profound it would wreck my entire life.

"Brenna, I just need you to know that lots of Christians wrestle with same-sex attraction, and I am really glad you're here." Jon then smiled, stood up, and walked away.

Are you stunned? This happened to me thirteen years ago, and I still am. It didn't make sense. Jon could have told me, "Marriage is between one man and one woman, and what you feel is a sin." He could have called me out on theology or threatened to tell my parents. He could have warned the other leaders and asked me to leave. He could have reminded me that a Christian religious program was the last place I should be and ushered me out.

Instead, he left room for me to be myself and expressed gladness that I, a struggling gay teen unsure of Christianity, was in that place with him.

The Collector of Taxes

I doubt you'll be surprised to hear that I "fake read" the Bible in church most of my life, even highlighting the right passages for the sake of fitting in. I was surrounded with its teachings, but I always struggled to see how that out-of-touch book connected with my life, my brokenness, my ruined soul.

Until the day I read—I mean truly read—a section of Mark 2 and was shocked to see myself in it.

Among the regular characters found throughout the Gospels, two groups of people were viewed in especially negative light in Jewish society: tax collectors and those known as "sinners." This is saying something, because both groups were typically Jewish and were, by birth, a part of "God's chosen people." But God's chosen people wanted nothing to do with them.

Ignored in the streets or slandered behind closed doors, tax collectors and "sinners" were viewed as being some of the worst of the worst. Tax collectors sold their souls to work for Rome, often abusing the power the ruling authorities gave them. And yet here is how Jesus interacted with one of the worst of the worst:

As [Jesus] walked along, he saw Levi son of Alphaeus sitting at the tax collector's booth. "Follow me," Jesus told him, and Levi got up and followed him. While Jesus was having dinner at Levi's house, many tax collectors and sinners were eating with him and his disciples, for there were many who followed him. (Mark 2:14–15)

As Jesus began His earthly ministry, news of His influence, teachings, and social interactions began to spread throughout the neighboring towns. Pharisees and prostitutes alike wanted to catch a glimpse of what this guy was all about. Given that many Jews presumed Jesus had come to destroy Rome, and that Levi worked for Rome as a tax collector, it's likely Levi hoped to avoid running into Jesus. So just think of Levi's horror as he recognized Jesus' gaze was set toward him.

I can't help but wonder if Levi felt the way I did when Jon found my eyes, asking, "Can I talk to you?" Maybe fear consumed him, too, as he felt unsafe.

The Sinners

I imagine some Jews watched eagerly, counting on the wrath of Christ to call out Levi for his iniquities. Finally, after years of taking advantage of poor Jewish families, pocketing unearned wages, and living out of the hand of a corrupt government, Levi would get what was coming to him. Jesus would condemn the life he'd been living and maybe even run him out of town. That's probably what was expected.

When all who surrounded a sinner far from God held their breath for his damnation, Christ left him room to be present—and

CAN I SAY THAT?

not just room, but an invitation to come closer. "Follow me," He said (v. 14).

Did Levi admit to his sin first? No.

Did he apologize for aiding in corruption? No.

Did he ask Christ to make him clean? No, at least not in that moment.

The call of Christ in Mark 2 is radical, offensive, and completely unexpected. In a time and culture where you only entered the temple and presence of God after purification, signifying a desire to live as God had called the Israelites to, inviting someone unrepentant and uninterested in the morally upright Jewish ways to spend time with Jesus would have been appalling. Jesus, however, wasn't looking for the morally "put together." Those were not the people in desperate need of Him. Jesus sought out those who had dug their own graves, who couldn't remove the tar from their bones, who were marked as incompatible.

> When the teachers of the law who were Pharisees saw him eating with the sinners and tax collectors, they asked his disciples: "Why does he eat with tax collectors and sinners?" On hearing this, Jesus said to them, "It is not the healthy who need a doctor, but the sick. I have not come to call the righteous, but sinners." (vv. 16–17)

Jesus was saying that it didn't make sense to call the clean when His entire purpose was to wash people white as snow. It didn't make sense to call the pure when His entire purpose was to blot out people's transgressions. So it doesn't make sense for any church today to make room only for those with clean, shiny, untangled lives.

When I recognized myself in Mark 2, I saw that Jesus invites *everyone* to experience Him. To sit down and have a meal with Him. To ask Him hard questions. And to do so *before* He requires our obedience.

The church hasn't done this well.

I haven't done this well.

But Jesus' example to us is *to leave room for everyone*. Jesus did not call Levi to the standard of being His follower before Levi got the chance to know Him.

Therefore, I am not calling you to the standard of following Christ before you have gotten to know the person of Christ. What I *am* doing is extending an invitation to you to step into the room Jesus is offering you as you turn the pages of this book. I am saying, come inhabit this space, but not with gritted teeth or your fake, on-guard smile or "right" answers. Come with your mess and your unedited language flowing. Dare to be your full self, like the tax collector who shared a meal with the God-Man.

Be willing to say that thing and ask that question.

Be okay with causing the religious leaders to question, "What is happening?!"

All I ever wanted was to be known. Jon came to know me and didn't demand my perfection. As he allowed me to wrestle with Christianity inside a Christian circle, rather than outside of it, I had room to take one step closer to knowing Christ Himself. Not the version of Jesus the Westboro Baptist Church painted, nor the version the metal-chair Baptist church drew . . . but the Jesus who eats with prostitutes and tax collectors.

The Jesus who creates safe spaces because of who He is.

The Jesus who invites you, just as you are, to step closer to Him.

CHAPTER 3

CAN MY HUMANITY LEAD TO HOLINESS?

I never got to the point in high school where I loved the amazing God everyone kept talking about. But I was good at pretending. I said the right things, stayed highly involved, and could pass as your regular Christian youth kid. I pulled it off, and I was exhausted. It's no wonder I held on to anxiety and anger to the point of self-destruction.

For me, that included an eating disorder. It wasn't only a way to cope with my less-than-favorable view of myself; it was also, for me, a path toward becoming someone worthy of love. Or just a version of myself I could try to accept.

Ever since I'd vacationed in Hawaii as a kid, I'd dreamed of living there someday. When I felt suffocated in my guilt-laced Christian bubble, I'd escape into daydreams about a future version of myself living in Hawaii. I would be super tan, unrealistically skinny, totally ripped from surfing, and strolling on the beach with a joint in hand. I might end up on a magazine cover with the headline, "Hottest Lesbian Surfer Ever." I imagined that the "thin, godless hippie" me would finally be at peace with herself and find relief from her torturous inner life.

Aching to get away from the constant pressure to perform Christianity, I had plans to go to college and live however I wanted to. My pitiful high school grades, however, were putting my dream of becoming a full-fledged heathen undergrad out of reach. So, with all the confidence of a decent liar and lazy academic, I gathered there was only one place I could go to run away from God. I would become a missionary.

My parents and leaders and friends were thrilled, of course, seeing it as another step in the life of a good Christian kid. I saw it as an opportunity to *get the heck out*, to go surf and smoke weed and be free. I would be hiding from God right under His nose, where He'd never care to look.

The moment I heard of a tiny missionary school in the hills of Haiku, Maui, I was the most Christian kid *ever*. My rehearsed Christian answers eventually landed me a spot in a six-month discipleship training school with Youth With A Mission (YWAM), which was 2,559 miles away from home.

When I looked in the mirror and saw a far cry from the trim, tropical hippie version of myself I'd imagined, I knew I had my work cut out for me. I became obsessed with losing weight in the months before I left for Maui.

It started out by skipping a meal here and there, then slowly rolled into expelling everything, even water, from my body at the end of the day. My dream life simultaneously seduced me and made me miserable. As I sat in youth group meetings, I couldn't help but wonder how God viewed what I was doing.

Even if God were loving, would He care that I am slowly deteriorating in order to look ideal?

It's just vanity—not that big of a deal, I'd reason. *Even if the Christian God is real, He'd never care about something like this.*

After months of treating my body terribly, I'd lie in bed at night and think, *My parents* have *to know. Or surely they'll find out at some point.* I wasn't sure if I dreaded or dreamed of an intervention. Either way, deep down, I sensed it was only a matter of time until my secret surfaced.

And when it did, would I be loved? Even though I'd be found so broken?

As I sat on the plane to Maui, it seemed like I was carrying enough baggage to drown me. I felt like an absolute wreck. Even if I did end up believing in God, what could He ever do with all my dirty laundry? All my bricks? All the mess of my humanity?

Leave Me Alone

As an extreme introvert, I'd been horrified to learn that I would have *seventeen roommates* in my living quarters in Maui. The moment my mentor, Lauren, heard this, she informed me her prayer for my time was that I wouldn't murder anyone. She knew me well.

To say I went into this training program with a chip on my shoulder or a bad attitude would not be going far enough. They might as well have renamed me April Ludgate or Wednesday Addams. I exuded serial killer vibes, with a touch of emo and "she might already be stoned." It's safe to say I was officially done with trying to fit the good-Christian-kid mold.

Here are a few highlights of how eighteen-year-old Brenna let her true colors fly at missionary training school.

1. A pressing question of mine was, "Is it a problem if I cuss, or is that fine? Are people going to be weird about it?"

2. When people became too friendly, I pulled out my weed shirt. It was covered with cannabis and pops of color that, when you looked closer, were actually pills. After I put it on, the room would get a little quieter.

3. I sometimes ached for time alone so much that I'd go float in the ocean for several hours at a time just to avoid conversation. The first time I did this, when I finally emerged from the water, someone called me a sea lion. (I'm sorry, a sea lion? She went on my hit list.)

The Shame Chair

The worst part of the early days of missionary school was the requirement for each person to tell their "God story" to the entire group.

The leaders dragged us out to the wilderness to camp out for days, and while we were out there, each leader took a turn sitting in a lawn chair and telling their story. (*Wow, very cool,* I muttered at the end of each one.) Then they dropped the bomb that we wouldn't leave until all thirty-one students had shared their testimony too. *Holy crap.*

It was unending agony. A lot of weird allegories and long-winded narratives. Boys offering incoherent mumbles, girls sobbing so hard you couldn't catch a word, all unbearably awkward. Add to this the bad meals, the poor sleep, and the awkward games, and I honestly figured we all might as well die out there. I'd had no idea social torture would be part of the program's curriculum and was deeply regretting my life choices.

I lay in my tent at night stressing about how to hide my eating disorder habits and trying to piece together my own fake God story—I mean testimony—for when I'd be forced to sit in the plastic chair of shame. Maybe I'd talk about being depressed; Christians loved a good depression story. I could throw in something about temptation (not my actual temptation) and end with a nice lie, like "I'm so excited for this season!"

I wonder if you've ever had a "shame chair" moment. I don't mean, "Have you concocted a fake testimony?" (although, who knows). I mean, have you felt like everyone around you was squeaky clean while you were covered in tar? Or like you were in a room where everyone knows something that you don't, and no one is trying to help you out?

So many of us have felt this in Christian circles. Maybe it was the Christian community you got kicked out of, or the "upstanding person" who looked down on you. We have had terrible interactions when we realized our "stuff," our *reality*, was not wanted in a place of faith. We have to stop and ask ourselves, *Does that accurately portray the heart of the God we find in the Bible?*

If we presented ourselves to Him with our baggage and bricks, do we believe He would run from us too?

"I Know God Cares About This"

The excruciating "shame chair" sessions continued. I was so bored out of my gourd from listening to typical church kids' stories that I might as well have been on Ambien. Then, out of nowhere, a voice shattered my apathy and woke me up.

A girl named Hannah looked mystifyingly relaxed as she smiled and shared about her life. As I (actually) listened to her speak, I couldn't help but wonder if this was someone I could be friends with, at least for the six months I needed to survive there. She wasn't obnoxiously loud or overly dramatic but seemed to be fully herself.

As I warmed to the idea of a friendship, a pair of words shot out of Hannah's mouth like an arrow and landed square in my chest. *Eating disorder.*

After blinking as slowly as possible, I felt my face become flushed with heat. Hannah had just given away *our* secret, only she was fine and I was not. I worried that people would start looking straight at me the second Hannah said the words. Surely they would know.

Listening to Hannah was like watching a sunrise; something drew me in even though I could predict what was going to happen. I knew she was going to say something about that man Jesus, probably something cliché, yet her tone was authentic. Where it felt like everyone else had forced out a fake revelation, Hannah simply spoke about her experience. As I waited for the nice little Christian bow to tie up the end of her story, perhaps, "and now I am healed!" or "I love Christ!" that wasn't what she offered. Instead she ended with piercing vulnerability.

"I am not really sure what God is doing," she admitted. "I still struggle, but somehow I think . . . I know God cares about this."

What the actual crap was that? I thought. *You mean to tell me you don't know what God is doing? You share one of the deepest struggles of your life* in the midst of still struggling, *and you have the audacity to claim that God cares about this?*

I probably stared at Hannah for two weeks straight trying to figure her out. I couldn't process the fact that she believed God cared about her eating disorder when I'd been convinced He didn't care about mine.

I watched Hannah walk out to the front yard in the morning to "spend time with the man Jesus." I saw her standing out from the other students; while they were unsure of themselves, she was at home in her own body. My eyes would be trained on her when she'd get back from runs, when she'd pull out her earbuds, crack a smile at me, and gently say, "Hi, Brenna."

I was waiting to see if I could catch a moment of unhappiness or fake interaction. I was projecting myself onto her, because I couldn't get over how different we—as two people who struggled with eating disorders—were.

While she was standing comfortably, I was trying to shrink myself down. While she was not anxious, I was a complete wreck inside. While she would leave a meal in peace, I was counting calories, thinking of the miles I could run, or deciding which bathroom I could throw up in. While she *knew* God cared about her body, I was beating mine into submission with the assumption that it had nothing to do with Him. My heart panged as I thought of a God who had created me but was now careless about the framework He'd put me in.

Meanwhile, the stunning, life-altering reality was this: Hannah was right. What was true for her was true for me, even if I didn't accept it.

I had no secrets before God. He could see every bit of me, all my faults, weaknesses, and screwups. He saw my attempts to hide myself, to cut myself off from people, to control my body. He knew me, completely.

I didn't have to hide my struggles; those didn't scare Him off. He knew me *and* He cared about me.

He didn't want me to become perfect or perform for Him. He wanted me to come close to Him and be real with Him.

This was the Father's heart toward me. But I couldn't see that, and I'd go on not seeing it for quite some time.

Hannah: God's Grace

By my third week in Maui, I was feeling miserable physically. It's hard to hide an eating disorder in close community, and because of that my body was experiencing the horror of having to digest food for the first time in almost six months. It felt like bone-deep discomfort.

Hannah continued to fascinate me, although the more I thought about her reality, the more I hated mine. How could God care about the carnal? How could the destruction of my flesh and bones be in the mind of the Creator? And how could Hannah, who once was in the same wreckage I now dwelled in, find her home at the feet of Jesus—a home not only for her soul but also for her physical body?

One day during a trip to town, Hannah and I were both walking the massive aisles of Costco. My rampant thoughts must have clouded my judgment, because I found myself charging toward Hannah out of pure angst.

"Hey!" I blurted out gruffly, with a volume that shocked us both.

"Brenna, hi," she said kindly.

In the silence that followed, I kept looking at her fiercely and desperately.

She leaned toward me with a warm expression.

Finally, I managed, "What did you mean when you said God cares about your eating disorder?" Six months of starving myself and a lifetime of not liking my body sat behind that question.

"You struggle, too, huh?" she replied.

I never imagined confessing a secret struggle inside a Costco, but I nodded my head as I clenched my jaw.

She invited me to walk with her.

I can't tell you that Hannah offered a clear answer to my question that day or in the weeks that followed. She never quoted verses or spouted out rehearsed words. Instead, she showed up, sometimes wildly, in my life over and over and over again, talking about the man Jesus.

A Coffee

October 28, 2014, was the first birthday I spent away from home in my nineteen years of life. I woke up to the normal clamor of community—showers running, alarms going off, heavy feet stomping through the halls—and wondered how many people knew it was my birthday. The information was posted on a wall somewhere, but who paid attention to those types of things? I always wanted to be seen without asking for it, seen because someone wanted to see me.

To my surprise, Hannah appeared by my bed and set down a cup of coffee next to me. It had two Splendas and a splash of almond milk, exactly how I made it every morning.

"Happy birthday, Brenna." Her words snuck out of her smile as she squeezed my shoulder, then she left as quickly as she came in.

Is this You seeing me, God? I wondered as I sat astonished at the small gift of being known. Coffee *exactly* as I would make it, physical affection, *and* minimal words? It was one love language after another for me.

Over the past month my time in Maui had been peppered with God's grace—with Hannah. I'd stand up from the dinner table feeling anxious, and I would catch Hannah's eyes and her face would say to me, *I know. It's hard.*

She'd catch me on the way to the bathroom, but instead of reprimanding me, she'd simply say, "Let's go outside."

Continuous small encounters stacked up in my heart almost to the height of my brick-made piles of rubble. I kept wondering *why* and *how* she kept showing up. Maybe she was watching me the way I was watching her? Maybe God had something to do with it? (I especially wrestled with that possibility.) It truly was odd, since Hannah and I had different rooms, different teams, and different daily schedules, and we rarely had time together. I figured that, even if God did not care, He wasn't actively stopping someone else from caring.

Hannah's continual recognition of my suffering created a tension in me, and after eight weeks of experiencing her care, I had to press the issue.

One day when our paths crossed and we got to hang out, we enjoyed a casual talk about what it'd be like to live in different countries someday. When the conversation came to a lull, the tension in me stirred in the silence. I pressed my lips together, looking down, hoping I could avoid the words that were aching to get out.

Hannah caught my eyes and waited.

"I just don't understand"—the words fumbled out of my

mouth with surprising emotion—"how you get to the place of knowing that God cares."

For two months, we'd all been spending hours every day learning about the Bible, the heart of God, Jesus, and the Holy Spirit. I could understand that God cared about the heart condition of His followers. I could understand that He wanted His children to make wise choices that impact our relationships and guide our emotional responses. But I still couldn't see how the torment of my physical body *mattered to Him*.

My eyes welled up with tears.

We were silent for a bit, then Hannah replied, "Brenna, our bodies were never meant to be a burden to carry. But now they are both broken and the temple."

We don't have to be struggle-free for God to come near.

We don't have to be faultless for God to rush in with His love.

Our baggage and our bricks won't stop Him from wanting to be close to us.

Wow.

When the Holy Meets the Unholy

Many of us assume God cannot tolerate our mess. After all, God is holy, and humans are bent toward sin—and if you've read the Old Testament, you know how serious holiness is. But the story of how unholy humans interact with the holy God progressed there, and sometimes we don't keep the whole story in mind.

But let's do a broad overview of that story now, since it can give us some significant insights about how God is reaching toward us today.

To be holy is to be without blemish or blame, without fault

or failure, completely sinless. God is the only perfect being in existence, the only Holy One.

His holiness is so forceful that it is dangerous to whoever is unholy. This is why He created methods for the Israelites to become "clean" enough (temporarily purer, really) so they could come *near* to Him. They repeatedly carried out rituals of sacrifice and followed strict rules so they could get closer to His holy presence for short amounts of time.

When people were not careful to carry out God's methods, there were terrifying results. Nadab and Abihu burned the wrong incense and died (Leviticus 10). Uzziah entered the temple in arrogance and left with leprosy (2 Chronicles 26). Uzzah, who attempted to do what he thought was right, but was in fact wrong, was struck dead (2 Samuel 6). While it's tempting to think, *This God is a maniac*, the truth is, holiness is deadly to those who are not holy.

That's why, when the prophet Isaiah received a vision in which he was in the Lord's presence, he cried, "Woe to me! . . . I am ruined! For I am a man of unclean lips . . . and my eyes have seen the King, the LORD Almighty" (Isaiah 6:5).

Then came a bizarre twist: an angel took a coal from the altar and touched Isaiah's lips, saying, "Your guilt is taken away and your sin atoned for" (v. 7).

When unholy Isaiah encountered the holy God, an angel of God cleansed him, and not just momentarily. No rituals or sacrifices were required. No immediate danger surfaced when the unholy encountered the holy. In fact, there was a *transfer* of holiness to the unclean.

And this was a picture of the new, mind-blowing possibilities Jesus would bring humanity.

What Jesus Made Possible

Let's look at what happened on the night of Jesus' death.

"When Jesus had cried out again in a loud voice, he gave up his spirit. At that moment the curtain of the temple was torn in two from top to bottom. The earth shook, the rocks split" (Matthew 27:50–51).

The curtain that had held back the presence of God from the people who desperately needed Him and rightly feared Him *dropped down*. It was torn in two, from top to bottom.

The holy was coming to the unholy.

It would make sense for us to expect a wave of death to fall over the people the second God's presence was unleashed; here was an unholy people unprepared and unworthy of being with a holy God.

But this was not so. No wave of death occurred, no plague of leprosy overwhelmed. Though the earth shook, not one human heart was harmed.

Why? Because the man Jesus made an exchange.

Throughout Jesus' earthly ministry He talked of a way that people could be *with* God, not by performing sacrifices or holding perfectly to the law, but *through* Him: "I am the way and the truth and the life. No one comes to the Father except through me" (John 14:6).

What a massive shock this would have been to those who came from generations of temple-centered people! Sacrifices, rituals, and rules at the temple—this had been their way of life for so many generations. Then Jesus became the last sacrifice.

And the physical structure of the temple was no longer the primary dwelling place of God. He would build a new temple—not as a place but as a people.

Now the Spirit Draws Near

Here's a verse you may have heard when someone was talking about sex or tattoos (it's always sex or tattoos, isn't it?) or maybe guilt-tripping you into eating healthier: "Do you not know that your bodies are temples of the Holy Spirit, who is in you, whom you have received from God? You are not your own; you were bought at a price. Therefore honor God with your bodies" (1 Corinthians 6:19–20).

There is a profound reality here that every created being should have to wrestle with: *Our bodies contain the dwelling presence of God.*

Through Christ's death on the cross, the new reality was set into motion. The temple with its torn curtain became obsolete as the Spirit was on the move.

It's exactly what Jesus predicted when He told His disciples: "I will not leave you as orphans; I will come to you. Before long, the world will not see me anymore, but you will see me. Because I live, you also will live. On that day you will realize that I am in my Father, and you are in me, and I am in you" (John 14:18–20).

This would become undeniably apparent when the events of the book of Acts took place—when people started seeing the Holy Spirit move in miraculous ways.

Still, it's easy for us today to read these passages about the inner dwelling of the Spirit and think, *It's just figurative. He doesn't really reside in my body.*

But why would we separate our humanity from the workings of the Trinity? Why should we assume that God only cares about our emotional, relational, and spiritual needs and is indifferent to our physical needs? Our Creator wove together all these aspects to form who we are. He clearly deemed the physical crucial to the spiritual. Case in point: we just read in 1 Corinthians that our bodies are a sanctuary for Him, the living God.

The verse preceding that passage underscores the importance of the physical, saying, "Flee from sexual immorality. All other sins a person commits are outside the body, but whoever sins sexually, sins against their own body" (1 Corinthians 6:18).

What we do with our physical bodies matters *because* they are our living, breathing, moving temples that house the Spirit of our Holy Creator.

A massive wave of death did not occur when the temple curtain tore. The opposite occurred. A massive wave of *new life* flowed into the people of God.

God chose to give us temple access now and anywhere through our flesh and bones.

Both Broken and the Temple

I cannot claim to have learned all of this as I sat with Hannah in Maui as a nineteen-year-old. Honestly, I am still learning to understand it today, in real time.

Nor was I set free of struggles concerning my body at that time. I would go on to have issues with sex and anxiety surrounding weight gain. I'd have incongruent feelings and a decent number of gray hairs before thirty. Today I feel too skinny; yesterday that was not the case. You and I experience the brokenness of this world daily in our physical bodies. We hurt, we hunger, we tire, we have limits.

But these twinges and aches do not negate what Christ has said, what God has done, or where the Holy Spirit inhabits. In fact, in radical resistance against the evils at work, God in His ever-redemptive Spirit finds a way to use our brokenness to bring us, time and time again, back to holiness.

We've covered a lot of territory, but here is the biggest thing I hope you catch: God asks us not to hide in shame, but to bring all our "stuff," our realities, to Him. All the dirty laundry we could ever pile into mounds of baggage, all the bricks we could carry on our backs. And with a great gesture of gentleness, He asks if He can have it.

We have to decide if we will hand our knotted mess over to Him. But if we do, He will not cast it aside like those who hurl shame. Instead, graciously and with great care, He will start to untangle our great heaps, because He knows He can use it.

He wants to bring His love to our brokenness.

He wants to bring His holiness to our humanity.

You might be reading this thinking, *I am nowhere near ready to bring my stuff to God.* That is completely fair. You might even be questioning if you will ever believe in the redemption of past pains and brokenness. Can I just tell you that holding those questions is normal and more than okay? Not only that, but you are in good company. I've been there, and many others have been too.

In the years after my time with YWAM, I continually wrestled in the tension of the broken and holy. Not without tears, I'd gather myself at a table to confront my food, my hunger, and my idea of "a good body." Palms pressed together, I learned to pray, *Lord, thank You for a body that functions and food that sustains. Would You be enough for me in the temptation and incongruent feelings?*

Praying that prayer wasn't as hard as living it, as aiming to let God be enough. It meant leaning into discomfort when I knew doing what I wanted would pacify the aches. I had to learn what God's voice sounded like and how to cry out consistently.

What once felt hard became only odd, and what once was odd became muscle memory. This new skill of reliance would bring me to Jesus day in and day out.

You can do the same, even in uncertainty.

Your prayer might sound like, *God, I don't know how You could ever use or redeem the brokenness I have carried, but in courage I want to step out and try giving it over to You. Would You help me to do that?*

Although this path has been difficult, I have never been abandoned there. I've found that when you're reliant on the Helper, your burdens are not your own to shoulder.

CHAPTER 4

WHY DOES YOUR PRESENCE FEEL SO LONELY?

The taste of Christ and freedom I received during my time in YWAM rippled through my life like a tsunami. It lit a passion in my heart that made the idea of not doing ministry virtually impossible. How could I stay silent after what I had experienced? How could I not try to give voice to the life-changing reality of Christ's intervention with humanity?

While I wasn't exactly sure what that would look like, I leaned into the opportunities I was given, first leading worship as needed, then leading a weekly small group, which eventually landed me a worship intern position.

Not only was my outward life changing, but my inward personal challenges were changing as well.

I had always dreamed of having a family. While I surrendered my sexuality and future life to Christ after coming to agree to live the way He calls all His followers to, I still continued to talk with Him about a future family.

At the same time, I had become quite close with Austin Blain, a young man who served at the same youth group as me. After writing letters to each other throughout my time in YWAM and then during his own six months away, we became bonded by ministry and travels as well as worship leading.

As months went by, I found myself asking the Lord, *Can You make sense of these feelings? I cannot help but want to do ministry with Austin for life—but how would that work? If this is from You, can You help me out with the "attraction" part?* I did not expect God to make me straight, and I can tell you right now that is not what happened, as attraction to the same sex is still a very real struggle for me. But I can tell you that as weeks and months went by, I started to experience butterflies in my stomach every time I saw those kind brown eyes. And with more prayers came more peace. I was falling in love with ministry, and I was falling in love with Austin.

At the same time, I started to believe that maybe, possibly, I was being healed. While self-harm and thoughts of suicide had started in middle school and stuck with me throughout high school, post-YWAM Brenna began to thrive for the first time in a long while.

Getting up was easy; I was motivated to go to work. I loved being around people. (Spooky, right?) And death? It hardly ever crossed my mind.

And so the way I talked about mental health changed ever so slightly. My struggles were no longer present tense; they were in the past.

I couldn't ignore what I was witnessing. Disbelief was no longer an option. I had seen what could only be God moving, rescuing, and restoring. So when He did that for me through small daily changes, I had complete confidence that I would remain in the land of the living. After all, in just over a year I had gone from a life of severe longing to fully healed of a darkness that had once been my home. I really thought I was healed.

Until I woke up two and a half years later, completely alone in a psych ward.

And the question consumed me: *Where is God when I am suffering?*

A Suicidal Pastor

The year 2018 should have been the best year of my life. I had just married Austin and had been miraculously handed a job running a youth ministry after a year and a half of interning. Between all that and working as a barista on the side, I sensed God asking me to pursue a Bible and theology degree. I know—me, who hated school! With a decent heart change toward ministry and a man, you might as well add this too. The fact was, with the opportunities I was getting to teach out of the Bible, the conviction to teach *well* crept in, so I threw school onto the pile of all the changes.

Everything about my life on paper was dreamy. But in real life I felt like I was trapped in a psych-thriller movie.

The anxiety started at the end of August 2017. One day in a grocery store, seemingly randomly, my heart began to race. I could not shake the feeling of dissonance that reverberated through my skin. With each day that passed, the feeling grew and evolved, eating away at my sanity one bite at a time.

By the end of September, I was back in counseling and back on meds. As I'd sit in my therapist's waiting room, legs shaking,

I'd talk to the God I thought had healed me: *I know You see me, and I believe You can heal me. So won't You heal me, Jesus?*

You probably know how weary the human heart can get while you are waiting. Between the waves of anticipation and letdown, you just try to keep yourself afloat. I prayed that prayer for 142 days straight. Every single night I would beg God for the ability to sleep, only to wake up after two hours.

Between preaching on Wednesday nights and leading worship on Sunday mornings, I started to feel like a walking failure. How could I look people in the eye and say that God is for them, only to turn around and think, *But He isn't enough for me*? I started to exchange trust in God for hope for relief in death.

This was real; I was suffering. I could not look at our hardwood floors without picturing my blood pooling over them. I couldn't take medication unsupervised or sit in the tub. The amount of times I sat with a belt around my neck trying to convince myself to tie it to our closet rung became countless as winter rushed on. Part of me was always thankful I couldn't muster the ability to do it, but that part of me was fading.

By January, I had lost ten pounds. I wasn't getting better—I was getting worse. Finally, I decided if Jesus wouldn't heal me, I could gather the guts to attempt to get myself into His presence. It was Sunday morning, January 14, 2018.

Have you ever found yourself in a pit of despair? With brain fog so overwhelming you could not fathom even attempting to explain what is going on inside? Maybe you ache to get it out, to share it with someone, but you know the doubt you hold would cause them to leave and the pain of that would break you.

Have you ever been sleepless in agony? Or unable to stop sleeping because it is the only time when all the pain ceases or at least pauses for a few hours? Maybe you found love and felt whole, and then they up and left. Maybe you lost the one thing you spent all your time praying for, and you do not understand how a "good God" could ever allow that.

I cannot help but think I have not been alone in this hellhole. You know, the familiar, dull pain of a long and looming dark night?

God is here with us, but He doesn't always heal, He doesn't always intervene, and He doesn't always promise earthly rescue.

So where does that leave us?

Woeful Mornings

I woke up staring at the ceiling. As I turned to check the time, my eyes scanned the room, and I realized I wouldn't be here for much longer. It was 2:45 a.m., and I was done living. Breathing slower than I ever have, I started to form a schedule and a plan. I had a worship night to lead in the evening and a meeting on Monday morning . . . but if I could leave work early that day, it would give me enough time. No one would be concerned about me if I showed up to things I was scheduled to be at, and if I could muscle through those, I would be in the clear. Austin wouldn't be home until evening, and if my attempt was unsuccessful immediately, time would take care of that.

That night I gritted my teeth as I sang the words, "Oh God, You never leave my side." I hated singing those words. I felt like a liar and a coward and an unbeliever, but mostly I felt holistically impoverished. I had no more faith, no more hope that God would take this suffering from me, no sense of rest. That night I lingered while hugging a few friends, pressing my hand firmly on their backs as if to say goodbye without words.

Morning, again. Two thirty in the morning. Austin slept next to me in the dark. I sighed and then remembered this emptiness didn't have much longer to torment me. I closed my eyes and prayed for strength, remembering that the moment of death would bring, in the very same instant, union with Christ. So even if it would be painful, that memory would pale in comparison to my new reality.

The time went by oddly fast, and I soon found myself climbing out of my car at the church office. It would end up sitting there for four days before somebody went and got it.

I set my stuff down on my desk and checked the time. My last meeting would be with Jon, my old youth pastor, who was now discipling me through my own season of youth pastoring. As I walked to his office, I remembered the day I had been offered this job. Jon had given me a charge: "I know mental health has been a struggle in your past, Brenna. If it comes up again, please know that we want to help you and be here for you. Tell us what you need if you need it."

I could take this final meeting to ask for help, but what difference would it make? What help could Jon or the church offer that God couldn't give? I walked in, eyes redder than in the previous months, and sat down quietly.

"I . . . I've been praying about stepping down from this role. I'm just struggling . . . and I feel like this is something I need to give up."

Jon didn't look surprised. He prayed with me and asked if I'd take two weeks to think and pray about it.

I said yes, knowing it was completely irrelevant. I stood and returned to my office to grab my things. I swung my bag over my shoulder to go home for what I expected to be the last time.

Waking Up

The room was floor-to-ceiling white, and so was the small bed, the only item in this space. A wide doorframe with no actual door showcased a metal prison toilet, sink, and showerhead. On the opposite side of the room, the door to the hallway was closed. A long rectangular window encased a set of blinds between two panes of thick glass with security wiring.

The intercom pinged. "Today is Tuesday, January 16, and it is 7:00 a.m."

I lay there in a pair of teal scrubs under a thin white sheet. A loud thud forced my head toward the noise of my door opening. A nurse with a clipboard and pencil said good morning without making eye contact, using her pencil to open the blinds on the strange window. I had never seen daylight like that before. Maybe it was the situation or the all-white room with nothing in it, but the beams absorbed all my attention. I forgot about my lack of underwear, my chapped lips, my missing hair tie, my phone, my car, my computer, my friends, my husband, my reality.

The nurse set down a towel, a sheet of paper, and a crayon, letting me know I could shower and mark my breakfast order.

"The crayon makes it safe, ya know?" she said, shrugging her shoulders.

Safe for what? I thought as I continued to drink in the surroundings.

It wasn't until she left that I started to remember. I stood in the strange shower, letting the water run right over my face, and my eyes burned as I pushed the wet hair out of my eyes.

This was the psych ward. I was alive.

How Did I Get Here?

Hot water covered the floor of the bathroom as I reached for my towel, trying to convince myself this was real life. I searched my memory and saw myself heading out of my church office when my office door abruptly opened.

And then the memories started rushing back, and I could see it all over again, how I had spent the day before, starting in my office at the church.

A short figure with shoulder-length brown hair turned, closed the door behind her, and sat at the only other chair in the office. It was Deanna, the mother of a friend, a woman I'd known for twelve years. If there was one quality that marked her, it was wisdom.

I expected a smile, but instead I was met with concern in her eyes and a tone of voice I hadn't heard from her before. She spoke intently.

"Brenna, do you need to go to the hospital?" This was not the conversation I expected or wanted or ever thought I would be having.

"No! No, I . . . I'm fine. I'm okay."

I tried to look convincing. It didn't work.

"Brenna, just think about it for a few minutes. Would there be any sense of relief in going to the hospital to see if maybe someone who knows what's going on could get you some help?"

By now my vision was blurry from the tears rolling hot down my cheeks. I sat there thinking for a bit. *What good could it do? But what bad could it do?*

Maybe I'm not crazy. Maybe thinking about dying every single day is somewhat normal.

Okay, probably not. But if I say no, there's no way Deanna will let me go home alone.

My plan isn't necessarily thwarted; it's on hold. I might as well get some stronger drugs for the in-between.

Without looking her in the eyes, I finally nodded yes. Before we headed to the hospital, Deanna fed me lunch and called Austin, who said he'd meet us there.

The ER was packed with crying kids and open wounds. As I walked into triage, I was asked what brought me into the ER today. I swallowed the lump in my throat.

"Um . . . I'm planning on killing myself, and I guess I came here for help."

Every time I said this throughout my six hours in the ER, the mood of the nurses instantly changed. Deanna and Austin sat close by while graciously giving me space to have these conversations. I'd then have to relay my plans and watch as my words contorted their professional countenance. I hated making people feel sad, but I wondered if my plans were decent enough to be lethal and if that's what caused the change in face. After several calls to different state hospitals, a caseworker finally found a psych ward with room for me.

Two tall, muscular men in all-black body armor stood by the nurse's station. I stretched my neck to see who was about to get arrested when they turned and walked straight into my room. I clenched my jaw.

"Ms. Blain? Are you ready to go?" It was my transport to the next hospital, about an hour and a half away.

When he realized my husband had stepped away to use the restroom, the man asked, "Do you want to wait a minute so you can say goodbye to him?"

"No," I answered, assuming I would see him when we arrived at the next hospital.

I was wrong.

We got to Longview around 11:00 p.m. They weighed me, took inventory of my belongings that would be locked up, and printed me new wristbands. I was then walked into a unit that reminded me more of a solitary confinement floor than a hospital. A nurse took a few more vitals, and I finally felt able to speak.

"My husband followed me up here in his car," I managed. "When will I be able to see him?"

The nurse looked at me with disappointment. "I'm so sorry, honey. We have very strict visiting hours, so you won't be able to see anyone tonight." That lump in my throat returned.

"Would it be okay if I just called him on the phone, then, to say goodbye and goodnight?" My disappointment grew.

"I am so sorry. The phone use is strict too." Her look of disappointment hit its peak. "Oh, Brenna. This is such a bad time to arrive. It's time for the shift to switch, which means I can't stay in here with you. It will be at least an hour before anyone else can come in and check on you, but I promise someone will as soon as they can."

By the time the giant metal door closed with a resounding thud, I was already weeping. Not because I wasn't dead. Not because my plan hadn't worked, but because now . . . I was completely alone. There was no one to talk to, not a single person. There was no phone to pick up, no app to get on, no TV to watch, no books to read, no pictures to look at, nothing. Never in my life have I experienced this type of isolation.

I wanted to die, and now I was emotionally and physically

secluded from everything and everyone I had ever known. My sobbing moved through my entire body.

Need

What do you do when you're filled with agony but you can't even kill yourself anymore? When there's nothing to take your life and no one to acknowledge your humanity? When not even the gates of hell will open to you, yet you're chained just outside . . . what in the world do you do?

I hung my head low, tightening all the muscles in my body, trying to will myself to pass out. I just needed something to happen, and then, like a billboard in the middle of the wilderness, I saw the words in my head: "With prayer, make your requests known."

That's it. Not a full verse or even an accurate paraphrase, just a short sentence flashed through my mind. With a stomach full of anxiety, I wept through the only words I could gather up.

"Jesus, You haven't healed me. But would You at least be here with me now?"

My eyes drifted closed.

The next thing I knew, my fists were clenching the hospital sheets. "Today is Tuesday, January 16, and it is 7:00 a.m." A wave of realization hit me as I recalled those words I had spoken the night before. A feeling crept under my skin and settled into my bones . . . a feeling I did not recognize. The feeling of being *rested*.

I frantically tried to remember anything before the intercom announcement, but I couldn't—because I had been asleep. For the first time in almost six months, I had slept through the night. How? Why?

Do not be anxious about anything, but in every situation, by prayer and petition, with thanksgiving, present your requests to God. And the peace of God, which transcends all understanding, will guard your hearts and your minds in Christ Jesus. (Philippians 4:6–7)

Peace. Pray to God, and He will give you peace. It wasn't until a few weeks after I had been released from the psych ward that I fully started to realize what had happened that night, but when I did, the newfound recognition never left my heart or my mind. I had spent months praying for God to heal my brain and soothe my incongruent feelings, but never once did I *ask God to be with me.* My mind had been so consumed with my want for comfort that I never stopped to consider if my earthly suffering might be part of a bigger intention. I had grumbled, not realizing that although the fall of humanity had taken health from me, God would not let it take communion from me. Because now, five and a half years out of that psych ward, bipolar diagnoses and all, I have come to know Jesus in a way I could never know Him without a need, without a thorn in my flesh. Even though I still struggle, I am deeply thankful for the redemption God has sown through my suffering. Why? Because the intimacy I have gained with Him and the comfort I have come to know wouldn't be apparent if I hadn't had these uncomfortable and incredibly human ailments.

But Isn't It Just a Lack of Faith?

You might read that sentence and be tempted to skip this section. I know, I know . . . theology . . . boring. But as your friend (We really have to be close to being friends now. I just shared that I got my underwear confiscated at a hospital . . .), I have been told at times that I must have some unconfessed sin or less than a mustard seed's worth of faith because healing is God's plan for all His children, as if to say, if it isn't happening, it's probably my fault.

Maybe you hear this and you think, *Really? Where the heck would they get something like that?* To which I have to reply: Well, the Bible! It is true that the biblical text speaks to confession and faith as prerequisites for healing:

> The prayer offered in faith will make the sick person well; the Lord will raise them up. If they have sinned, they will be forgiven. Therefore confess your sins to each other and pray for each other so that you may be healed. The prayer of a righteous person is powerful and effective. (James 5:15–16)

In James alone we are told faith makes a sick person well and confession leads to healing. So what are we missing? Have I missed some unconfessed sin or lack of faith? I acknowledge that this really could be true. But while James 5 might not be wrong, it doesn't tell the whole story of healing and human suffering. We find a different nuance in the Bible's stories about the life of Paul. He wrote,

> In order to keep me from becoming conceited, I was given a thorn in my flesh, a messenger of Satan, to torment me. Three times I pleaded with the Lord to take it away from me. But he said to me, "My grace is sufficient for you, for my power is made perfect in weakness." Therefore I will boast all the more gladly about my weaknesses, so that Christ's power may rest

on me. That is why, for Christ's sake, I delight in weaknesses,
in insults, in hardships, in persecutions, in difficulties. For
when I am weak, then I am strong. (2 Corinthians 12:7–10)

It might not seem significant stripped of context, but I
marvel at Paul's faith in response to his suffering. Paul was
writing to a church community he had started years earlier
that had been inundated with leaders preaching a false gospel
(2 Corinthians 11). While these false teachers appeared to have
much to boast and brag about (maybe even faith that healed
instantly?), Paul appealed to his church community with a
word on how weakness clarifies God's strength. Paul was saying he, a more-than-faithful-and-committed follower of Christ,
asked to be healed, but God's plan to show Paul how powerful
and good He was in the face of weakness was so much better.
If this was God's will for Paul, why couldn't it also be His will
for some of us?

And if my strength was faltering, the faith of God's people
was holding me up. When I look back on this story in my life,
I am moved to wonder as I consider how, from the instant I
decided I would take my own life, the Lord was on the move to
preserve it. It is within the details of this story that I cannot deny
how God cares for us, sees us, and is with us, and I want you to
know that too.

On the Sunday night that I led worship for supposedly the
last time, my dad showed up. My dad and I didn't go to the same
church, nor did he feel comfortable at my church, so when he
walked in I was completely puzzled. Afterward I said hello, and
he told me he was praying for me. When my parents came to the
hospital the next day to see me, my mom told me that, in worship

that morning, my dad had said the words, "She's no longer a slave to fear, for she is a child of God."

Even now when I write that, I cry. God was moving him to pray for me.

When I asked Deanna how in the world she'd decided to show up at my office that day, she told me about discerning the Holy Spirit. "I was driving home and felt like I needed to pray for you, so I just pulled over and prayed. When I was praying God told me, 'Go get her,' so I did."

And perhaps most startling, after my shower and breakfast the first morning in the psych ward, I met with the psychiatrist. He came in, long white coat and all, looked at me, looked at my chart, and asked, "Are you a YWAMer?"

In shock I asked why the heck he would ask that, and he laughed when I told him he was right.

"You've got something you need to do. You're going to be a speaker, right?"

Okay . . . so he's a prophetic psychiatrist, or at least one with immense discernment. After that he reminded me that suicide doesn't fit into my theology, but a good stewardship of our suffering does. Remembering this even now still leaves me speechless. God worked to keep me alive, and He is doing the same for you. Why? Because God does not exist "outside" of our suffering. He is right there with us. How? Through the working of the Holy Spirit, through the fruition of God's will, and by the obedience of His people. Could you recognize in my story that God being *right here with us* so often means that we experience God through the faith, action, and literal presence of other believers? My dad, Deanna, my health-care providers . . . the list goes on and on. As odd as it can seem, we really do experience Him through and within humanity. We know the Holy Spirit through the body of Christ. God uses countless means and measures to let us know with great volume, *You are not alone.*

Maybe you don't fully believe yet, and that's okay—I still struggle too.

But if I can leave you with one thing, it is this: *He is with you.* He's with you not despite your suffering and not outside your suffering, but He is *in it* with you, communing with you, remaining next to you, holding you. He knows the pain, He knows the hurt, and He knows you.

And in His goodness, He is sorting our bricks, which He can see so much better than we can and knows how they can be used.

He does not cause your pain, but He does desire to redeem it and use it for something worthwhile and beautiful. You may not believe that today. You may deny it or doubt it. You may want to believe but do not find yourself there yet. *It is okay* if you are in any of these positions today.

But can I intrigue you to consider voicing where you find yourself right now . . . to God?

The conversation may surprise you.

PART 2

WILL YOU SHOW UP?

CHAPTER 5

ARE YOU JUST KEEPING SCORE?

You know that scene at the end of *Grease* where John Travolta thinks he's changing his lifestyle to get the good girl, but then out walks Olivia Newton John in tight black leather from head to toe, smoking a cigarette? I saw that scene for the first time when I was three years old, and all of a sudden I was awakened to my purpose in life: to be bad. Really bad.

My mom said that soon after that, she frequently caught me pretending to smoke when I was "playing house" with my friends. (It's something I can hardly wrap my brain around now when I look at my own four- and two-year-old children—I can't picture them doing that.) No one had to teach me how to sin, and certainly no one had to convince me that it is what my flesh wanted. I was completely on board.

I would spend the next sixteen years of my life actively chasing sin and the thrills of my heart, convinced that the term *sin* was just a long list of forbidden things God kept tightly in His hands. He was probably constantly checking it and anticipating the moment I'd trip up. Every now and then the confusion between guilt and conviction would cloud my brain, and I would start to bargain: *God, I will stop cutting if You just take my depression away. I won't do it ever again.*

Then I would end up back in that place of debt, missing the mark of what God has called His people to. I wondered if sin was just something He'd made up to hold against us.

Have you wondered this too? Did God create standards He knew we couldn't meet? Does He just keep score of our screw-ups? Is He the kind of god who is just out to catch us, criticize us, punish us—a cruel tyrant?

A False Picture of Sin

The term *sin* is triggering to some and vague for others. You might have grown up with this word being thrown at you like a grenade; being called a *sinner* was the ultimate inducer of shame and could lead to exile. Maybe your faith circle of origin led you to believe there was a difference between "church people" and "sinners." The church people were shiny and clean and had their act together, and the sinners seemed—dare I say?—kind of normal.

Throughout my entire childhood, I thought R-rated movies were the worst images anyone could ever put into their minds. I imagined they were chock-full of horrific, violent sexual acts and bad words I had never heard. I assumed they resulted in instant trauma for the viewers. So imagine my surprise when, at seventeen years old, I saw my first R-rated movie and realized: this is just *real life*—the words I heard every day, the body parts I knew existed, the tumultuous relationships that I witnessed while living in the real world. It felt like the "evil" I had been sheltered from was my everyday life. Either the sheltering had been a bit much, or my life was one that others should be sheltered from.

This false picture of sin is one that I call *selective*. It is the idea that sin only impacts the worst, the dirty, the broken—but not the churched. You know, not the pastors, not the youth group kids who over-participate. Not the people who never cuss or the ones who look shocked when they smell weed. Not the people who shop at Nordstrom instead of Hot Topic. No one from private schools or on the honor roll.

You get the picture: check certain boxes and you pass.

The bricks created by these fallacies are so misshapen that they lack the ability to uphold any sound structure. It is paramount that they be given to Truth, to Christ, to be reshaped so they may be used.

Because at their core, these faulty ideas contradict what we see in Scripture. The book of Romans tells us, "There is no difference between Jew or Gentile, for all have sinned and fall short of the glory of God, and all are justified freely by his grace through the redemption that came by Christ Jesus" (3:22–24).

Paul, a Jew, wrote these words to a group of Gentiles, or non-Jewish people, making it clear that people who grew up with the Jewish Law (like Paul) were just as guilty as those who did not (like the Gentiles). The Jews, no matter how they presented themselves, were not really shiny, clean, and sinless. And the Gentiles? They were not less deserving of redemption and community because of their family or culture.

All people—Republicans and Democrats, MDivs and high

school dropouts, single dads and trophy wives, fast-food workers and CEOs, sex workers and health-care workers, pastors and prisoners—all have fallen short. The best and kindest person you know is just as sinful as the person in your life who has hurt you the most. There is no hierarchy where sin is concerned. It levels all of us.

What Does Sin Do?

I am sinful and you are sinful, and that is a huge problem. Catastrophic, actually—because sin separates us from the Holy One.

Remember back in chapter 3 when I mentioned the transfer of holiness that took place during Isaiah's vision? Isaiah entered the temple and realized that he, an unclean man of sin, should not be in the holy presence of God. But shockingly, instead of being destroyed, Isaiah *was made holy* (Isaiah 6:1–7).

This vision, however, was not a foretelling of the extinction of sin. It was not suggesting that people in later generations would gain Christ and therefore no longer deal with impurities that keep them from perfection. Rather, it was a picture of what sin does and what people like us can do with it in the wake of Christ's death and resurrection.

Isaiah's fear and expected demise tells us of the actuality of sin in our lives. It keeps us from the very person who created us and knows what's best for us. It stains and infects and makes us unworthy of being in the presence of the Trinity.

Imagine longing for the arms of Home but never being able to get there because of your heart's condition. The longing creates anguish, and in anguish we live, aching for the impossible.

That is what sin does. It keeps us from going Home, from experiencing God's best. It plugs up our ears so we can't hear the Holy Spirit and keeps our backs turned from the Father. Sin chooses Barabbas over and over and over again while Christ willingly goes to our death over and over and over again (Matthew 27:15–26). Satan wants you to think that sin is where we end, that Jesus' body was placed in the tomb and nothing more.

But Isaiah's vision did not leave him in fear; it left him in awestruck wonder. In what world does the reality of sin also exist with a reality of awestruck wonder? The one we are living in.

Read that again: *the one we are living in.*

Isaiah got a vision of what you and I are invited to do, any second of any day, over and over and over again.

Forgiveness of sins. Absolute cleansing. Being made holy as He is holy. Welcomed in. Crafted into the temple. A wild, wild truth.

Where sin casts us out and away, Christ brings us in and holds us close.

Where sin leaves us nameless and labeled, God calls us by His name.

When sin meets the person of Christ, it crumbles.

Isaiah spent his entire life living from sacrifice to sacrifice to maintain atonement. But us? This vision Isaiah received gave us a glimpse of the immediate forgiveness of sins and complete banishment of our guilt that Jesus brought. Not guilt in the way of feeling bad, but guilt as in *blood on our hands, guilty in a court of law.* We deserve the punishment for sin, but Jesus—the only person worthy of declaring forgiveness because of the perfect life He led—pardons us completely.

I want us to sit, as much as we humanly can, with the weight of that. Think about how often we extend apologies and get the reply, "It's okay." Or how often we are wronged and the best thing we can get out of our chest is, "It's okay," said with a slightly bothered and sad tone. We feel the pain of what has been done to us or what we have done to others, and that pain compresses us.

What if Christ's reply to us was, "It's okay"?

But no, it's not okay . . . !

What is His actual response to our earnest recognition of our wrongs?

"I forgive you."

Can we try and synthesize the reality of what this looks like? Imagine that, after a day full of distractions and stress, you get behind the wheel to go home. You are exhausted and probably should not be driving, but to you it's just the end of another day. Then the unimaginable happens. You close your eyes for a moment and the next thing you know, you're being charged with reckless driving, maybe even manslaughter. The evidence is there, you even plead guilty—but the judge? He looks at you long and hard with some sort of astounding kindness in his eyes. And as both sides wait for the verdict everyone expects, the judge only says one thing.

"I forgive you."

Instead of awkwardly walking out of that courtroom to go sit at home in the what-ifs, depression, and isolation, imagine if the judge then invites you to his house for dinner. You talk for hours, and he listens, looks you in the eyes, and smiles warmly. When it is time to go, he asks if he can swing by tomorrow to check in on you. Weeks go by and he still stops in every day, and you start to maybe consider him to be a friend.

Look at where you started. Look at where you are now. Once

guilty, now daily in the presence of the judge who has become familiar and, dare I say, a comfort.

He has shown through action that he deeply cares about your well-being, about you being seen, known, and understood.

Even more, he wants you to be liberated from the habitual actions that got you there.

He shows up *to help.* Not to condemn, not to damn, not to walk away.

What Does Shame Do?

While I remained in the closet during most of my high school years, I noticed the space in there started to shrink as I collected garbage bags full of sin and shame. Have you ever thought about how often those two words go together: sin and shame? While I would ignore my reality as best I could, I was experiencing what much of humanity has experienced since the start: indulging in sin that brings on the stomachache of shame.

In Genesis 3:7–11, Adam and Eve were shocked into a new reality in the wake of their sin. Realizing their nakedness for the first time, they covered their bodies with clothes and attempted to hide from God.

God replied with a question: "Where are you?" (v. 9). He, of course, already knew the answer; He was prompting them to confront their sin.

Adam and Eve felt the first embodiment of shame brought on by sin. Shame had two specific impacts in this narrative: first, their realization of being naked; and second, their choosing to hide.

Today, shame has the same effect. It causes us to realize the

disordered and broken things in our lives, and instead of holding
security in Christ, we suffer insecurity. We cover up things and
gloss over them. Shame tells us that being hidden away is better
than being found out, so we hide when we do wrong.

Some of us know the pain of being found in our wrongdo-
ing: we have been met with guilt and more shame, and we have
even been sinned against in return. It is no wonder that our feet
know how to carry us the fastest when we come to realize what
we have done.

When I feel shame I tend to push people away. I text less,
engage less. I don't reach out to my friends, I avoid social outings
that I would normally enjoy, and I don't hang around waiting to
be approached.

What do you do? Maybe you overcompensate? Maybe you
punish yourself? Whatever it is, all of humanity attempts to dis-
tract or conceal. You, me, our friends and family—we all have
desperately worn the camouflage sewn by sin.

But no amount of running and hiding can keep us from
being found out. No number of days, weeks, or years can separate
us from our reality. God's Word makes this abundantly clear.

"You may be sure that your sin will find you out" (Numbers
32:23).

"There is nothing concealed that will not be disclosed, or
hidden that will not be made known" (Luke 12:2–3).

"For God will bring every deed into judgment, including every
hidden thing, whether it is good or evil" (Ecclesiastes 12:14).

These are just three examples out of several dozen that all
communicate the same thing: God knows, and God will be
just. There is no hiding anything from our omniscient Creator,
whether we hail Him as that or not.

Now, this can do two things for us: it can terrify us, which I believe it should, and it can also destroy our shame, if we let it. Why? Because God is unlike any other being we have ever known.

Let's look at a story He gave us that puts this on display.

What Does God Do?

After living approximately two decades of life and blowing all his money his dad gave him on reckless, sinful living, a young man is brought to his lowest point—his pit. Unable to earn money for food and with no one to turn to, he finds himself dumpster diving just to stay alive.

He realizes with horror the bridges he has burned by taking his family's money and leaving. And the shame now attached to his name. Sex, money, gambling, scandals . . . and now nothing. He betrayed his family and built a personal legacy of selfish acts and guilty living.

He considers the anger and disappointment he would rightly face if he were to return home. The likelihood of his father ever considering him a son again would be nil. But he is hungry and has absolutely nothing. He decides he would face that anger— and a lifetime of servitude—just to be regularly fed.

For several days and nights he travels back home on foot, contemplating what each step means. He anticipates apologizing for what is unforgivable, seeing the brokenness he has caused, and facing pain and possible hatred. *But at least I will be able to survive*, he thinks.

As he nears his father's house, a deeper humiliation sinks in. His breaths start coming more quickly as an uproar of emotion takes over. Now it is becoming real. The exposure and weight of every sin he committed, every heart he broke, every lie he told, every dagger he left in the backs of those who raised him—they are unavoidable. He has sinned against the only people who have ever truly loved him.

Before he can cover his mouth to mask his guttural sobs, he hears a familiar sound. Feet, running on the dirt road, getting closer and closer. Out of embarrassment he starts to wipe the snot and tears away while trying to hold in the loss of air, but it's too late. He hears a voice he recognizes: his father's, calling his name.

He braces himself for a rage born of injustice. He imagines the trial that will determine his sentence, but even a lifetime of servanthood would never repay what he has done. His mother will never smile at him again. He'll never taste her food or feel her comfort. His brother will never playfully tease him throughout the days; he won't even be permitted to sit with the family at meals. And his father . . . he will most likely never hear his laugh, and the voice that told him when he was growing up, *You are safe, and you belong here with me.*

All this flies through his mind as his father approaches. Eyes tightly closed and muscles tensed, the son is ready to receive a beating he greatly deserves.

But instead, he is enveloped in the arms of his father and his feet are lifted just slightly off the ground. His father weeps.

"My son, I have been waiting for you to come home."

This is what being found by God is like. Even in our sin and hiding, God is unlike any other being we have ever known.

I invite you to acknowledge this at a deeper level with me. Would you take a minute and read a passage from Psalms out loud? It's something I need to do; I am in constant need of having to remind my soul who my Maker is and what He does in the wake of my humanity.

Let's read:

> Praise the LORD, my soul,
> and forget not all his benefits—
> who forgives all your sins
> and heals all your diseases,
> who redeems your life from the pit
> and crowns you with love and compassion,
> who satisfies your desires with good things
> so that your youth is renewed like the eagle's. . . .
> The LORD is compassionate and gracious,
> slow to anger, abounding in love.
> He will not always accuse,
> nor will he harbor his anger forever;
> he does not treat us as our sins deserve
> or repay us according to our iniquities.
> For as high as the heavens are above the earth,
> so great is his love for those who fear him;
> as far as the east is from the west,
> so far has he removed our transgressions from us.
> As a father has compassion on his children,
> so the LORD has compassion on those who
>   fear him.
>
> (PSALM 103:2–5, 8–13)

Our God is a Father who holds compassion for the least deserving.

Our God is a Judge who redeems the most reckless of lives.

Our God is a Friend whose slowness to anger affords us repentance.

Our God is like a Mother whose love abounds through selfless giving, time and time again. Shame cannot stand in the presence of this God.

May we remember this in our hiding and run swiftly toward Him in the same moment of remembrance.

Confession and Community

It is one thing to consider looking at our sin with God; it is quite another to look at it with other people. The very thought of this might freak you out, and I get that. But hang with me here.

I am not sure how many times Lauren, my mentor, dragged me to Target during middle school, but it was a lot. While most people in mentor situations would meet for coffee, Lauren always asked my mom if we could actually go do things. By the time I was fourteen, I had been tricked into eating wasabi, visited her and her husband's youth group that they pastored, gone on zoo trips, looked through her photo albums (with all her strange outfits and hairstyles from the previous decade), baked dozens of cookies, driven through Starbucks entirely too many times for living in the Pacific Northwest, learned what a latte was, and watched *Mean Girls* while asking forbidden questions about (yikes!) sex. The point being, Lauren and I never really sat down across from each other to talk; we did things together.

When life got hard and I started to make some poor choices, I realized this habit could actually benefit me.

I had been self-harming for around half a year when

I finally considered talking to her about it. I wasn't looking forward to the conversation, considering every other interaction I had experienced when people found this out. Shock, crying, and disappointment seemed to be the only fathomable responses the few who knew could muster up. But when I realized I wouldn't have to look Lauren in the eyes if I told her about my self-harming on our monthly Target trip, I thought I could probably gather up the courage and at least endure the anger or crying.

I still remember every detail—my throat getting dry when we walked through the automatic doors, her asking how I was doing while she grabbed a red cart and began to push it toward the cereal aisle, and my heart pounding when I knew that was the one natural opportunity I would get to share.

I forced the words out, and then my ears rang.

"Hmm." Lauren continued to push the cart and then called attention to some random article of clothing. She looked at me briefly, smiled, and continued walking.

"Why do you think you have been having a hard time lately?" Then she just listened.

I was stunned. She was so calm. So gentle. So gracious.

And this experience of confession completely changed my life.

Often, at least in the Protestant church, when we think about confession we think of legalism or old traditions. We believe we should confess to God, but when it comes to those around us in our spiritual communities, we often fall silent. But confession is a necessary and blessed spiritual practice.

Something significant happens when we confess out loud to our brothers and sisters in Christ. And while it may be a nerve-wracking practice to think about, consider where we, the collective body, have come from.

All of us, every single one of us, has been the prodigal son. We all have run, hidden, wept, and returned in shame to be met by the deepest of loves—the sacrificed Son who bled for us. He doesn't just wait; He runs into the road when we are far off. He calls our names and longs to look us in the eyes while welcoming us home.

Being met in the middle of the road—being met by Graciousness Himself—changes how we meet others.

While Lauren seemed to have been born with an innate sense of grace for others, she wasn't. Her experience with Christ, the way she was met in confession by others, and her growth in the Holy Spirit all enabled her to meet me the way she did.

And those gifts are not far from us; they are readily available to all God's beloved.

The book of James is unique compared to the other New Testament letters. Instead of being addressed to one specific church, like most of the letters written by Paul, James is a collection of insights to all Christian believers. So the following words James wrote were not meant for one particular congregation but *all Christians*: "Confess your sins to each other and pray for each other so that you may be healed. The prayer of a righteous person is powerful and effective" (5:16).

When we step into the practice of confession, we aren't just setting an example for followers of Jesus; we are operating out of obedience and faith toward God.

While not all sickness and suffering are caused by sin, confession to one another and prayer can, in some cases, relieve sickness. If it is a possibility to be gifted with relief from Christ, why not try? I am not sure that confession has ever led to physical healing in my life, but it has brought about real change.

Confession between God and me still leaves me with agency to continue doing wrong, but public confession invites accountability.

For thirteen years now, I have been confessing to Lauren. Some of my greatest shames have been relieved by her consistent and grace-filled reply, "Thank you for sharing with me," even in the face of some pretty gnarly sins. Not only do I get the relief of speaking them into the light, but I receive the shepherding of someone older and wiser, who can recognize, infiltrate, and disrupt the patterns in my life that have given birth to these sins.

The invitation to confess our sins to one another is active combat against the Enemy and our flesh. It is hard work, but it is also work that leads us to spiritual and communal wholeness.

New Life

This kind of experience with confession can feel impossible in "clean" church spaces. Before I experienced the graciousness of Lauren, I'd witnessed only the tight-lipped testimonies that seemed to have passed through a car wash before reaching the public ear. They were edited experiences that went along with edited teachings from Scripture, which led me to believe that no one, not a soul in the church or character in the Bible, *actually struggled* in the ways I did. It made me feel completely alone in my sin, and I came to view it as an impossible situation, something I'd never be able to work through.

Until I read the Bible for myself.

As someone who wrestles with same-sex attraction, I have

read and heard all the verses that condemn homosexual relationships. Most of the time, they are ripped out of their intended context.

Now, I know that sentence can cause some uneasy feelings, so let me tell you what I do and do not mean.

Typically, people love to use 1 Corinthians 6:9–10 to call out the sinful and separating behavior of those who have found themselves giving in to the same temptation I face. But why not quote the entire section? What type of message does the easy one-liner present versus the passage as a whole?

> Do you not know that wrongdoers will not inherit the kingdom of God? Do not be deceived: Neither the sexually immoral nor idolaters nor adulterers nor men who have sex with men nor thieves nor the greedy nor drunkards nor slanderers nor swindlers will inherit the kingdom of God.

It always has been strange to me that we use this passage to call out same-sex intimate behaviors, but we typically fall silent on the sins listed before and after it. Imagine what this says about what we believe and what it does for our witness! We cling wholeheartedly to a biblical sexual ethic but hesitate to say something to our Christian friends who consistently drink a little too much. We preach about a biblical sexual ethic but cover up the slander and swindling done by our pastors. We pick and choose.

Some might nod their head in agreement and suggest that, because of this, we should just throw out the whole list—but abandoning the biblical call to holiness has never been the answer.

Instead, we have to look at what comes next in the passage:

That is what some of you were. But you were washed, you were
sanctified, you were justified in the name of the Lord Jesus
Christ and by the Spirit of our God. (v. 11)

Washed, sanctified, and justified—in the name of Jesus, by
the Holy Spirit of our Father.

Paul looked at this church, this body of people he had come
to know and love. He recalled their history, their personal stories. Those who used to be temple prostitutes, those who used
to be abusive masters, those who used to be sought out for the
hottest town gossip, those with great amounts of wealth they kept
only for themselves—the list goes on. But the one thing all these
individual people had in common was a wild encounter with the
truth of Christ.

They came to know and believe in the salvation He gives—
and when they received the Holy Spirit, their lives started to
change. They no longer sought wholeness in sexuality or escaped
into drinking. They no longer gave themselves over to anger
and hatred. Their hearts grew in compassion and generosity, all
because the Holy Spirit was at work in their lives as they invited
Him to do so.

And the same Spirit is alive and available to us today.

It is not, nor has it ever been, about willpower. I did not hand
over my freedom to love whomever I want because I muscled
myself into submission. I did not surrender my freedom to get
drunk because of a bargain I made with God. And I do not
continue on the narrow path because of wildly compelling
apologetics.

Why have I given up these things (that have felt really good
to my flesh in the past) and asked the Holy Spirit to infiltrate my

life? Why am I constantly praying to be searched and known and led away from offensive ways, as it says in Psalm 139?

Because I was met on the road.

In my sin and shame and iniquities, I was embraced by the most provocative display of love.

The one who died for the undeserving and sat with the outcasts ran toward me, and He runs toward you. He gives His very own Spirit to us and invites us to step into holy living with Him.

When our affection lies in the arms of Christ, walking away from sin suddenly makes sense. Surrendering our fleshly desires makes sense. Bearing our crosses well makes sense. Listening to the Spirit makes sense. Becoming tenderhearted, gentle, and gracious people becomes possible. The point is not the "rules," but rather the relationship.

Will you open your heart to the Father who has run out into the road to meet you?

You don't have to start with your sin. In fact, you can't; you first must come to know the person of Christ. Only then can you decide whether He is worth following.

If your answer is yes, know that the Holy Spirit will carry you, remind you, and guide you. It will be difficult, but it will no longer be impossible.

The apostle Paul reminded his friends of this truth in Galatians 5. He clearly said that they'd have desires that contradicted God's desires, but they were not left on their own to tough it out. The Spirit would help them. "Walk by the Spirit, and you will not gratify the desires of the flesh," he explained (v. 16).

If God was a dictator or even just a glorified teacher, giving us rules and then seeing if we got it right, would He give us His Spirit? No. Instead, He gives us a helper who works to contradict our flesh. He reminds us to lean on someone beyond ourselves—and that someone deeply cares about *us*.

God does not desire to scrub us clean so we may appear "put together." He desires to help us out of our mess and hurt so we may find true freedom in Him. It is not about the rules. It's about the relationship.

It's about getting our heart condition healed so we can come back to the arms of Home.

Feeling the awestruck wonder of being cleansed and made holy, of always, always being welcomed in.

Not plugging up our ears, so we can hear His loving, joyful voice.

And not letting our backs turn away from Him, so we can see His face and know who our treasure is and where we belong.

CHAPTER 6

ARE YOU LISTENING TO US?

I wear socks with my TOMS shoes. I know that's kind of weird," said the skinniest boy I had ever met.

I stared at him, unsure of how to respond to such a strange sentence, so I said nothing, and the two of us proceeded to sit in complete silence until it was time to go. I was fourteen and angsty, and it was my first time playing on this youth worship team, which happened to include this kid who had no idea how to talk to people.

Almost every week for the next four years I would see that boy at youth group or community college and remember his name. Sometimes we would share a wave in the music building or end up in the same larger groups for games at youth group, but we never exchanged words. Seriously, over four years the one conversation we'd had was one sentence long and on the subject of socks; that was it. I'd eventually gather that he was an extremely kind kid, but I couldn't have told you anything else about him.

So how did this kid end up going from only existing in the far-off corners of my mind to being the person I now wake up next to every single morning?

Through a series of unfathomable occurrences. What is more surprising is what those occurrences ended up revealing to me about God and my own struggles with connection. But let me tell you first about falling in love. While I gave some of the broad strokes of how Austin and I grew close earlier, I'd love to share more of how we became "us."

Just Encouragement

On October 28, 2014, I had just finished my afternoon YWAM work duties when a leader told me a package and a letter had arrived for me. It was my birthday, so I wasn't surprised to receive a bundle from home, but the letter was a mystery. When I picked up my mail, I instantly recognized my mom's comforting hand-writing on one of the packages. Gifts from home. But the letter was from Austin Blain, the boy who'd only spoken to me once four years ago. Why on earth was he writing me a letter?

After opening my package from home and FaceTiming my family to say thank you, I cautiously opened Austin's letter. Inside were six sheets of notebook paper carefully folded into thirds. As I read through each one, I heard Austin's voice for the first time.

He was kind. He started off by sharing how he'd seen a post about what I was up to with YWAM and thought missionaries could always use encouragement, and he had prayers and words to give.

He was thoughtful. Each page poured over into the next as

he quoted applicable Bible verses and explained how he felt like they might come in handy during my months away from home.

He was generous. He offered a listening ear and a promise to write back, should I need someone to talk to. I was stunned. In what world did a college-aged boy have and actually take the time to handwrite a letter of encouragement to someone he didn't even know?

I fell out of touch with almost everyone back home besides my parents over those six months. The Lord was changing me so drastically—I'd gone from hating church to devoting myself to ministry—and I was unsure how to talk to my friends who only knew the old me. When I'd tried to ask them questions about God, I was often met with silence or a shrug. With the distance, it did not seem to make sense to try any harder. Despite that, I still had a deep desire to process with people who would be around when my time with YWAM was done, and there was one person who was willing to listen. Austin Blain.

Writing back to him for the first time felt so incredibly odd. I desperately wanted to ask, "Hey Skinny, do you still wear socks with your TOMS?" but I knew starting with sarcasm was not a wise choice. So I just started with the truth.

I am being changed by God.

It was both scary and safe to be so vulnerable with someone I did not really know. Sure, Austin knew my name and where I was in the world, but he didn't know the things I'd struggled with throughout high school or that my youth group years were mostly fraudulent.

But the kindness in his first letter hinted to me that he also might be a person of graciousness, so the truth flowed out of my pen.

And it turned out he was a person of graciousness.

For five months Austin and I exchanged handwritten and emailed letters that covered every topic under the sun. Thoughts about theology and healing, worship music, favorite podcasts, best places to get tacos in Portland, best Christmas memories from childhood, what our respective plans were for the week, and prayers we started praying for each other.

It was not long until I realized that I not only knew Austin, but I dearly loved him. Not one moment of our conversations had been face-to-face, but he had become one of my most treasured friends.

When I returned home, Austin and I spent six months actually eating tacos in Portland together, going to church together, leading worship together, and doing various other activities face-to-face.

But, no—we weren't dating. While my heart had grown ridiculously fond of Austin, the peace surrounding the idea of dating was not there. And this was not because of my sexuality and struggles, but because he'd be leaving to have his own adventure with YWAM soon. It made my heart ache. Yes, I was gay and the feelings I had for him were complicated at best, but my heart longed to be near him.

When he left, we resumed our ritual of letter writing, and this only brought us closer. While time together in person had been incredibly fun, it also had been filled with the distraction of *doing*—watching movies, playing games on our phones, reading books, going to arcades. Our focus on doing those things didn't foster emotional closeness like our letters did. But once our communication was focused on knowing the other person, our relationship changed again.

Then came the day when Austin would leave his YWAM base for his outreach location. He would be spending three months evangelizing in the mountains of Nepal, where internet and computer access would be spotty. I knew the expectation of even talking once a week was too high, and I was miserable.

I wandered around shopping aisles with my mom while the sinking dread of disconnection with him started to overwhelm me. Before I knew it, tears were streaming down my face, right in the middle of Walmart, because—there was no denying it—I had fallen in love with Austin.

I wouldn't be able to see him for weeks upon weeks, and the whole time I'd be aching to be near him. I felt like I belonged with him, I wanted our hearts to be connected, and now there would be an ocean between us—dark, swirling waters that meant days of traveling without a shared word. It didn't feel possible that I could feel close to anyone with that reality between us.

And yet, love overcame me.

It did not matter that I could not physically see Austin in the room; he reached out, and I knew he wanted to hear from me. We found ways to connect across that huge ocean. We did end up having regular communication after all, enough that I even found myself telling him at one point, "I trust you enough to want to spend my future with you."

As I look back on this now, I'm stunned at the beauty of it. All those conversations led to significant choices—to start dating, to get engaged and then married, to go back to school and work in ministry, to have kids, to buy a house. All those conversations built our relationship and the story of us.

And I'm struck by how this mirrors the way we build a relationship with God. Many conversations over time, no matter how mundane or emotional they feel, add up to a significant relationship.

Into the Void

For much of my life, praying felt as useful as tying notes to helium balloons in hopes of communicating with an astronaut. I'd squeeze my eyes shut, hoping that the concentrated force would somehow project my wishes, anxieties, and fears to a far-off God. A God who sat in the clouds with a giant beard and booming voice who might as well also only ever say one sentence to me and then cut off all communication.

This picture of God being far from me left a specific lens on my view of prayer. I prayed only on occasion—when I'd burst out a desperate plea and shout about my great weight of worry. My prayers became frantic and few, and I was dropping them into a vast void, not really toward God at all.

Maybe your lens is different. Maybe you feel like prayer is a bargaining tool, so you find yourself promising God certain behaviors in exchange for answers.

Or maybe prayer to you is strictly ritualistic and repetitive, and anything outside of what you have been taught feels wrong.

Maybe prayer feels like a one-way radio, where you're constantly talking but never hearing; even when you try, it's all static noise.

The bricks we have collected concerning prayer may feel small, like just a broken piece the size of a pebble in the bag surrounded by much weightier masses of brick. But I believe they have significant value.

If you don't, though, I understand.

Whatever our view is, let's fully acknowledge it and look at how it was crafted by our upbringing and environment. We all have come across poor teachings on prayer. We all have held misinformed views, mostly because they haven't been poked or prodded yet, so it would make sense for us to wonder if prayer is just an empty tradition, a waste of words. Or, if it is not, is there a wrong way and right way to do it? How can we know if we are doing it right?

Maybe better questions are, What is the point of prayer? Why does God ask us to do it? Is it a demand out of narcissism to hear more about how great He is? Or some strange sadistic pastime when people ask for healing God knowingly won't give? These are the questions that led the first eighteen years of my prayer life.

What about you?

The void that I used to pray into looked an awful lot like the Pacific Ocean that separated me from Austin when I was first with YWAM, from Washington state to Maui. It wasn't until I experienced that emotional intimacy with Austin from a separate continent that I came to see how powerful communication "from a distance" can be.

Although we do not currently have Jesus in the flesh with us face-to-face, we still have a God who longs to hear from us and a way to communicate with Him.

Did you know that He really wants to hear from you?

Your words can be jumbled, the tone wobbly. A prayer can be as short as a text or as long as a novel. You can voice your current aches and pains, your doubts and fears, or read Him the lyrics of a song you wrote. The content does not matter as much as the one producing it. God cares to hear from *you*, in your tone, from your heart, with your mannerisms and character and experiences, however knotted up they are. He knows that they'll never get untangled unless you hand them over to Him, in all your heaviness and anguish.

How can I be so sure? I know this because I have read the prayers of the man called "the one after God's own heart" (1 Samuel 13:14, author's paraphrase).

David

If you want to talk about someone with unsafe questions, we need to talk about David. The youngest of eight, David found himself with the luxurious job of babysitting livestock. That's what he was doing when he was first told that a throne he was never in line for would soon be his. Considering that the current king was later his best friend's dad, and a tormented king at that, you could sense some drama would make its way into his life.

Throughout the book of 1 Samuel, we are told that David killed a giant with a slingshot and a stone, was almost murdered by Saul (the king at the time), became king over Israel, commanded a married woman to sleep with him, got her pregnant, killed the woman's husband, mourned his newborn's death, and found out his own son had raped David's own daughter.

If anyone wondered if God cared enough to listen to them, *to really listen*, it would be David. Plagued by mistakes that the modern-day church would run from, one could only imagine where he even would begin a conversation with God. But we do not have to imagine, because we are given many of them word for word in the book of Psalms.

Take Psalm 51, for example. It's David's prayer after he was confronted about his affair, abuse, and murder. "My sacrifice . . . is a broken spirit" (v. 17).

Psalm 3 is David's prayer as he fled from his son who turned in rebellion toward him. "LORD, how many are my foes! How many rise up against me!" (v. 1).

And Psalm 22 holds David's words of utter despair, which Jesus Himself quoted when He was crucified on the cross: "My God, my God, why have you forsaken me?" (v. 1).

The more I think about it, the more radical the Psalms become to me. Smack in the middle of God's Word to us is a book full of the messiest confessions, deepest heartache, and real, visceral doubt. Admissions of sexual sin and murder. Heartache about generational sin that started with David himself. Doubt that God was still with David in his darkest night.

God saw it necessary to include these utterings, these cries, these screams in His holy Word. Why?

Because they matter.

Every emotion felt, every thought penned, every tear cried, every sin seen and unseen, all the contents that bubbled their way out of the human heart to the ears of God hold weight in His eyes. Because they are from His creation.

He feels the exact same way about you and me.

Hear My Own Mess

Maybe you hear about David and you think, *Look, he is a Bible dude and I cannot relate*, or you wonder if the "super-committed" Christians ever pray the raw, flagrant prayers you find yourself trying *not* to pray. I don't know if I can answer that question for you, but I can share a bit of my own doubt-filled prayers I have uttered in the darkest nights.

After four short years of marriage and just two months after my first miscarriage, I found out I was pregnant again. And then I started having symptoms that could indicate a second miscarriage.

For me, letting go of hope has always been easier than holding on to it, and so I quickly assumed I was indeed having a second miscarriage. As we waited for blood test results to tell us what was happening, family members and friends asked how they could pray for us. I said I only needed comfort; that was it. They prayed for this, but they also prayed for a healthy pregnancy.

To my surprise, the results came back showing that I was still pregnant.

An ultrasound at eight weeks confirmed a strong heartbeat but also a large hematoma. While most small hematomas in pregnancy are relatively harmless, the size of mine made it a threat and a possible cause for another miscarriage at any time.

With nothing to do but wait, I continued to ask God only for comfort and not hope for the best-case scenario, even as people continued to pray. I have always believed in healing. But after walking through what I have been through, I stopped asking. Besides, prayer has never been something I have understood well.

At twelve weeks I opted for a genetic screening via ultrasound so I could get another look at the size of the hematoma. As I chatted with the technician, she gently reminded me that most hematomas don't start to shrink until around fourteen weeks and to not be surprised if it was the exact same size.

But after a good twenty minutes of measuring and moving

and squashing my bladder, the technician looked at me with an oddly cheerful smile and declared, "I can't find the hematoma! A doctor will still need to double-check, but it's totally gone."

Hmm. Interesting. That was the extent of my reaction.

Why? Because I hadn't been praying for a miracle; I'd been praying I wouldn't pee my pants. I'd been praying that *when* we lost another baby I wouldn't be totally crushed. I was praying sensible, safe prayers. Good prayers.

But other people weren't.

Time flew by as I was busy parenting our precocious Rudy Saint Blain, and before I knew it, I was back in that ultrasound room for our twenty-week anatomy screening. We learned that a second boy would be joining us in August. With that same cheerful smile, our technician declared everything appeared to be looking good but that a doctor would need to confirm. Later that day I posted an ultrasound picture of little Rory holding his middle finger up to the ultrasound wand (he has my genes).

Then two days later everything changed.

After examining our ultrasound, doctors had discovered blood on Rory's brain. They couldn't tell if he had hemorrhaged or had a stroke. Whatever the case, this called for a whole new health-care route—specialists, a counselor who specialized in infant loss and grief, weekly ultrasounds throughout the remainder of my pregnancy. We'd have to keep trying to figure out what Rory's needs were and how to meet them.

I held back tears as we explained to our church community group what was happening. At that point, though, that's all I could really stand in terms of sharing; I wasn't ready to tell more people. But the few who knew about it prayed for healing, and every time they did, I slightly rolled my eyes.

Every morning I would wake up at 5:50 a.m. and walk for an hour, all the while talking to the Lord about how I could love and serve Rory however he came to us. Not once could I bring myself to pray for Rory to be healed, to receive a miracle. Not because I didn't believe God could do that, but because I didn't believe that was His plan for us. The fact was, Rory *was* sick. Why pray for healing if I could just pray for faithfulness? For courage? For strength?

The next ultrasound session was especially thorough—the technician took detailed measurements and pictures for about an hour. Rory was dancing the entire time. With every movement, I wanted to think he was okay and that it was all normal, but the thought of him moving because he was in pain wouldn't stay out of my head.

After the technician was done, Austin and I waited for the doctor to come in and report on the detailed findings. I thought about our sweet boy, whom I knew from the inside out and whom God knew from before conception. What would his life be like? How long would he live? What could God do with this tiny life, with our grief in the unknown, and with the collective cry in prayer?

The waiting time stretched from fifteen to thirty minutes. I held my breath. How bad could it be?

Then it stretched to ninety minutes. Horror and terror were the only things I was feeling by then. We should have been in and out by that point.

Within one office visit I had more ultrasound pictures of Rory than I'd had of Rudy over my entire pregnancy with him. Had they printed out a ton of them because these were possibly the last pictures we would ever get of Rory? I thought about the new counselor we would be seeing and the MRI I had scheduled. I wondered if a C-section would be less stress on his tiny body and if I would even get to hold him in the minutes after he was born. I wondered if he would be able to smile, hear, see, or laugh. My mind wondered frantically until that door swung back open.

"Well," our doctor said with wide eyes, "I am not really sure what to say to you guys."

In her hand she held a printed ultrasound picture and pulled up another on the screen.

"This is your ultrasound from last week. All this gray stuff—here—is blood on his brain. That's what it is."

We already knew this, so I was not really sure why she was showing us again. Then, pointing to that day's picture on the screen, she stared at the image for longer than what felt normal and looked back at us.

"And this . . . is from today. There is nothing. Here's another angle, still nothing. Here are eight more pictures that all show nothing. I have . . . no idea what happened. But there is no longer blood on your baby's brain and everything else . . . looks normal. Again . . . I don't know how. So we will continue to meet for follow-up ultrasounds just in case."

After eight more weeks of weekly ultrasounds, it was concluded that Rory was completely healthy.

We asked one question after another, but there was no logical explanation for this change. *Could it have been a faulty machine?* No, they used this one every day on several women. If it was faulty, this wouldn't have been the only case. *Could the matter have been a different medical issue?* Nothing that they had ever seen.

What struck me the most was the way the doctor behaved when she came to tell us the blood was inexplicably gone. Her hands and voice were shaking. This was *not normal*.

When I think about this miracle and my doubt, I think about a story in John 4 about a father who charged through the crowds toward Jesus, in desperation for his son who was about to die, who "went to [Jesus] and begged him to come and heal his son" (v. 47). I think about my own son and the only prayer I could pray for him in those horrendously long months, one filled with fear, pain, and doubt. This is what I wrote:

> *I am the father with the hurting son, full of anguish for what I cannot fix. No amount of running or trying has produced any hope. I am worn down by the longing and lack of understanding I wrestle with here, in the now and not yet.*
>
> *I come to You and ask one thing, like the father full of anguish.*
>
> *I believe You are who You say You are. I believe, for I have heard Your gentle, still voice. I believe, for I have stood in the wake of Your relentless peace after horrific life storms. I believe, because I have seen Your nail-torn hands.*
>
> *But my faith falls short.*
>
> *I believe, but my heart remains fickle.*
>
> *I believe, yet my words fall silent. My soul loses hope. My mind wanders away. So come help my unbelief, like the father full of anguish.*
>
> *I believe that in my unbelief the Holy Spirit groans and begins to fill in the gaps that my own faith could not*

bridge. I believe that in my unbelief the Father is interceding for me at Your right hand.

I believe You are enough. When words fail, You do not.

I believe; help my unbelief.

I brought Him my anguish, my doubt, and my desire for more belief.

I came as I was.

But most of all, I came close to Him.

No Matter the Means

Maybe it is easy for you to imagine the slow building of love and affection that comes with devoted conversation, but you cannot fathom a God who desires to hear from someone like me, with a truckful of doubt, or like David, with a string of big failures. Why would a good God allow the utterings of such tangled humanity in His presence?

Maybe, like me, you have felt so overwhelmed by fear or shame or unbelief that you've thought, *I am too messed up. My situation is too awful. Nothing will ever change. I can't picture God wanting to hear from me now.*

But let's go back to David. Somehow, in all his constant struggles and adulterated sin, he knew he could turn to God and he chose to do so. Why?

I believe it is because he came to know the nature of the Lord. David came to know that Perfection Himself was and is the only One equipped to deal with his messes, his wicked heart, his broken spirit. And this shaped the way David chose to approach God.

David could not get any more broken. And he could bring all his brokenness to the feet of God. Nothing was off-limits, because every dark and dingy corner needed the light, which could only be provided by the God of the universe.

Over time, David came to know the real change that resulted from running to God over and over and over again, instead of running away.

Just like falling in love through constant communication, the repetition of running to God in our biggest and smallest failings can sway our heart in a better direction. Why? Because no matter what brings us to God, it leaves us in His presence. This is why I believe the "pebbles" of prayer we have collected can actually be used as cornerstones.

Prayer, no matter the catalyst for it, takes us to God. It drops us off, with all our dirty laundry, running mascara, pockets full of drugs, bodies covered in bruises, whatever it may be, at Christ's doorstep. And that is the only place where change and comfort, peace and healing, rebuke and redemption, reconciliation and rest can take place. And that is the whole purpose of prayer.

Prayer is meant for communion with God. The definition of the verb *commune* is "to communicate intimately (with someone), esp. at a deep level of mental or spiritual engagement."[1]

I think a weird part, if you have grown up as a Christian, is having to unlearn the "religion" of prayer. So often I have felt like prayer had to sound a certain way, when really God was primarily looking to commune with me.

When we have a God who calls us to just *be with Him*, there

---

1. Oxford English Dictionary, s.v. "commune (v.)," accessed April 4, 2024, https://www.oed.com/search/dictionary/?scope=Entries&q=commune.

is so much freedom in what sharing our intimate thoughts and feelings can look like. Not just on Sundays, not just in thanksgiving. But in grief and turmoil, in the middle of your toddler's tantrums, or when your car breaks down. After you have been unfaithful, or before you spend the rest of your day cursing under your breath.

The act of going back to God time and time again impacted David because he gained a clearer understanding of the character of God. He started to see that He is slow to anger and abounding in steadfast love and that He forgives our sins (Exodus 34:6–7). *This* is why David was called a man after God's own heart—not because he was faultless, but because every time he screwed up, he ran swiftly to God's presence through prayer. He knew God was the only one who could meet every need he had, so he made prayer his first step of action.

Through that habitual practice of running to God, David's heart became eager for redemption. Prayer invites us not only to recognize our own and others' brokenness, but to taste and see the wholeness offered through Christ.

So pour out the contents of your heart. The ugly, the angry, the depressed, the doubt, the fear, the hate, the aggression, the failure, the pain, the sin; every piece of your humanity is welcome—because if it brings you to communion with God, God can and will use it. He just wants to hear from you.

CHAPTER 7

IS IT YOUR WORD AGAINST THEIRS?

Whenever I slipped out of my room as a kid, maybe because my stomach hurt or I needed a glass of water, I'd always encounter the same scene. Inside my parents' bedroom, my mom would be sitting by her bedside lamp, poring over the pages of her Bible. Still, today, if you go in at the right time, you will find her with her lamp lit and Bible open.

In high school, my mom's nickname was "Bible Bethany," and it was earned for good reason. She was never legalistic, though, and that's why her faith intrigued me. As much as she read the Bible, it was never a habit she forced on her kids. Sure, she read *The Message* out loud to us a few mornings a week while we were homeschooled, but there was never a voiced expectation that we had to read the Bible.

My mom's present yet covert faithfulness to the Bible was a stark contrast to much of the Christian world around me. At

Sunday school and Awana (a kids' Bible club), the focal point was never understanding what the Bible said but simply being able to regurgitate it word for word or checking off the boxes for the most number of days you actually read it.

Whether my perception is accurate or not, I can tell you that the methods used when I was in elementary school led young people to view reading and studying the Bible as a chore.

If that wasn't dreadful enough, when the Word was taught prescriptively and memorized outside of its proper context, it was easy to think it said something it didn't. But why would we expect our modern minds to easily understand an ancient book in ancient languages?

Misused, Abused, and Misinterpreted

Can you think of moments in your life when the Word was used prescriptively toward you? When well-meaning friends or family tried to engage your present struggles with biblical answers that just totally missed the mark?

For me, that started in middle school.

Middle school sucks. Your body is changing. You're experiencing feelings and emotions brand-new to you. You are becoming deeply socially aware while somehow also becoming deeply socially awkward. You might cut all your hair into a rat tail with a bad dye job so now you look like a raccoon. Not me, though . . . anyways.

These were the years the first twinges of mental illness hit me: racing thoughts, sleepless nights, and feeling horrifically empty. I remember receiving well-meaning scraps of Scripture from my friends and leaders who wanted to pacify my pain.

Do not be anxious about anything.
Cast all your cares on Him.

But whenever the words swirled around my ears, I felt my body growing ever numb to the ancient writings penned by people who could never know what it was like to be me.

Maybe you, too, have experienced people trying to use the Bible as a Band-Aid for your lacerations. Maybe someone has lunged at its pages in response to your shortcomings or stirred up a random verse as an "answer to prayer." Or maybe you have experienced the horror of people using the Bible as a weapon against your humanity. Or maybe you have just been offered poor interpretations and translations of the Bible that have led you to question how your reality could be so off base from what others would say "God has for you."

From the prosperity gospel to "God hates f*gs," it is both incredible and atrocious how humans have missed the point. With all this abuse and misinterpretation, how could we ever view the Bible as reliable and true, let alone good for us?

It took what felt like ages for me to even start to believe that the Bible is *good* for humanity. Before I could, I needed to deconstruct the harmful ways I had seen the Bible leveraged throughout my life and the history of the context in which I live (the evangelical West). For so much of the Bible's history, it has been made what it truly is not.

Let's talk about a few of those things the Bible just isn't.

The Bible Is Not a Band-Aid

"We know that in all things God works for the good of those who love him, who have been called according to his purpose"

(Romans 8:28). As an adult, I find the Word to be a constant comfort, but I still cannot hear this verse without shuddering.

I once sat in a small group, trying my best to open up about the odd mess my life had been since I had been molested and my parents had separated. It was only a matter of seconds before some trigger-happy, Bible-knowing girl flipped open to Romans, and I already knew where this was going.

"Brenna, I just really feel this for you right now."

I am sure my face gave away the absolute rage I was feeling, but the socially unaware middle schooler continued.

"You might think these are bad things happening, but God planned all of this for you!"

How could I argue with the Bible? *If I really loved God*, the words seemed to say, *I would accept that everything that had happened was for my good.*

At the time, I did not have the theological framework to say, "Actually, I believe it goes against God's character to say that He has caused my suffering." I was a hurting, confused kid, and someone was using the Bible to "cover up" my unsightly human wounding. I'm sure it was easier for everyone there to sit with that Bible verse than with my raw emotions.

Infuriatingly, this was only one of many occurrences. People continued to sling Bible verses at my brokenness as if it were wet plaster on a setting cast, hoping it would aid in the healing. But it never did, because the Bible was never meant to be a Band-Aid.

The Bible Is Not a Magic 8 Ball

Whether it is Philippians addressing anxiety or Romans talking about our future glory, the Bible cannot be spliced into pieces. We cannot apply Scripture based on key phrases or micro ideas that "feel" applicable to us. To really understand the meaning of the Bible, words and passages must be taken in their entire context, and that requires study. Sure, it is easy to shrug our shoulders at the thought of having to give time to understand what this book is really saying, but consider this:

Have you ever prayed, *God, show me what You want to say*, and flung the pages open, hoping to find something relevant to your life or situation? I have. But almost every time I'd land somewhere in the middle of Leviticus, and I would roll my eyes, thinking, *Yeah, this is great for the next time I need to practice animal sacrifice.*

It is easy to laugh, but we have to acknowledge how real this practice is. We ask the Holy Spirit to miraculously show up and hope that we will stumble upon something of worth and value. But the Bible isn't a Magic 8 Ball.

To break us of the habit of misuse of the text, we have to commit to good exegesis, which is just a fancy word for "critical thinking through the text." We can do this by asking questions like:

- Who wrote this?
- Who did they write it to?
- What was going on at the time when this was written?
- What was the culture like?
- What were common practices of the people who this narrative is about?
- What is the purpose of this book as it has been set within the whole Bible?

Although it takes time, practices like this help us gain clarity on the snippets of Scripture that have been commonly taken out of context.

Take Romans for example, where we find that verse (Romans 8:28) that has been used to ill effect so many times. When we jump into studying the book, we will find that Paul was addressing a church that had become divided over Jewish and non-Jewish practices, and his overall intention was to encourage this specific church to become unified.

In chapter 8, Paul talked about the gift that has been given to all believers (both Jewish and non-Jewish), the Holy Spirit. While Christians would still suffer in this life, Paul's emphasis in Romans 8:28 was not that God afflicted them with suffering in order to follow through with His plans. Instead, Paul was explaining that even within a broken world where people are given agency to sin and be the masters of their own lives, those who are in Christ can know God is working and will continue to work out their salvation. Context is everything.

The Bible Is Not a List of Rules

As a child of the '90s, I lived through the tail end of one of the strangest movements of Christianity in the Western world: purity culture. If you are unsure of what this means, you are fortunate. From my own experience and perception, purity culture was a movement of Christians who took Paul's and Jesus' guidance around sexual activity and created boundaries around the boundaries. The most egregious sin you could commit was sex before marriage, because sex meant everything.

People who committed to living out the principles of purity

culture often wore rings that pledged their virginity to their future spouse. (I wonder how many people who did that ever prayed about considering whether marriage was God's plan for them in the first place.) They often would give up "dating" for "courting"—you know, like the Amish—and would save their first kiss for marriage.

None of these things are outright wrong, but neither were any of these practices encouraged by Paul or Jesus. It was just a strange and arbitrary list of rules, and in turn many people who were introduced to purity culture adopted the mentality that the Bible itself was just a big book of strange rules.

While the Bible is full of commands we are to hold in our hearts, its entire message does not call us to follow a list of rules to be made righteous in God's sight. Within the Old Covenant (where the Israelites were given the law to follow) obedience does make you righteous. But the New Covenant (that God will forgive sins and therefore give the opportunity for right relationship with humanity) was necessary because it is impossible for us to obey.

The Bible is first and foremost the story of God entering into community with us, His children, and the ways in which He pursues humanity. The commands laced throughout Scripture are given to those who already have entered into relationship with Him, and we follow them from a place of trust and affection for Christ (as opposed to purity culture, where action was often seen as a way to gain affection from Christ).

We trust that He has our best interests in mind because He is who He says He is. If Christ is perfect and holy and good and loving and omniscient and to be revered, if He is incapable of sin and is the Maker of our souls, then the healthiest and best possible choice we can make is to yield our wants to Him and submit our lives to His biblical commands.

The Bible is not a list of rules; it is a shovel that uncovers the sinful condition of our hearts, uproots us from our sinful selves, and replants us within God's will and safety.

The Bible Is Not a Weapon

"You know you are going to hell, right?"

A dear and well-meaning friend asked me this as we swung on her hammock just minutes after I'd confessed my same-sex attraction (which I'll refer to as SSA) toward women. We had been raised in similar faith circles and, while our churches did not specifically teach this as truth for SSA individuals, the silence they held allowed the louder voices on the news to disciple our thoughts on the subject.

Homophobic churches led us to believe that all people had to live by the standards of Christ before getting to know the person of Christ—and if they didn't, they would burn in hell. Fear, created by a narrative of Scripture that lacked the impact of Christ's character, made the Bible into a weapon. It told people to "submit, or else" without ever touching on the *goodness* of *who* they were to submit to. Jesus said as much to the Pharisees.

> Hearing that Jesus had silenced the Sadducees, the Pharisees got together. One of them, an expert in the law, tested him with this question: "Teacher, which is the greatest commandment in the Law?"
>
> Jesus replied: "Love the Lord your God with all your heart

and with all your soul and with all your mind." (Matthew 22:34–37)

While a Band-Aid Bible and a Magic 8 Ball Bible are trying to be helpful, and a rule-book Bible is trying to "win" grace, perhaps one of the worst ways the Bible is abused is through the weaponization of twisted meaning. From slavery to mistreating SSA folks to forced marriages and covered-up abuse, people have taken the sacred words of the biblical text and contorted their meaning for personal and institutional gain.

Let's take a look at some of these examples.

In 2018, the Southern Baptist Convention (SBC), one of the largest Christian denominations within the United States, published a seventy-one-page document confessing that their denomination was literally founded on the basis of owning slaves.[1] While Northern Baptists denied slaveholders the privilege of being appointed as missionaries, many Southern Baptists argued slaveholding to be "God-ordained," most commonly citing Ephesians 6:5–9 to show favor toward slaveholders.[2] The SBC themselves have made a large effort to acknowledge their sin and apologize for their past abuses.

But those abuses go on.

In a 2009 interview, well-known reformed pastor John Piper responded to a question about how Ephesians 5:22—which teaches that wives are to submit to their husbands—applied to

---

1. Tom Gjelten, "Southern Baptist Seminary Confronts History of Slaveholding and 'Deep Racism,'" NPR, December 13, 2018, https://www.npr.org/2018/12/13/676333342/southern-baptist-seminary-confronts-history-of-slaveholding-and-deep-racism.

2. Dave Miller, "Slavery and the Bible: How Shall We Respond?" SBC Voices, March 13, 2023, https://sbcvoices.com/slavery-and-the-bible-how-shall-we-respond/.

women in abusive marriages. He explained, "If it is not requiring her to sin, but simply hurting her, then I think she endures verbal abuse for a season and she endures perhaps being smacked one night and then she seeks help from the church."[3]

Nowhere in this segment did he mention how the call for husbands to love their wives, which we see in Ephesians 5:25–30, would fully bar a husband from abusing his wife. Nor was there mention of seeking legal intervention from authorities or psychological help. This un-nuanced view leaves wives at the mercy of their husbands and church elders, many of whom are not qualified to handle issues of abuse like police officers and counselors are.

While the idea that humanity could engage in such an act of weaponizing the Bible is heinous and slightly unfathomable, we have to remember where the temptation to misapply Scripture came from in the first place.

In Matthew 4:1–11, Jesus retreated into the wilderness and was tempted by Satan—and what did Satan use to make his case? *God's very own words.* Three times, Satan took the good and upright words of Scripture and wove them into his attempts to lure Jesus toward temptation, each time implying a different meaning than the writers intended.

When we understand the overarching narrative and the character of Christ, we can know that, while the Bible does cut away sin, it does not cut through the dignity of humanity. The

---

3. John Piper, "John Piper: Does a Women Submit to Abuse?" posted September 1, 2009, eaandfaith, YouTube, 3 min. 57 sec., https://www.youtube.com/watch?v=3Ok -UPc2NLrM; excerpted from John Piper, "Confronting Emotional and Verbal Abuse in the Home," Ask Pastor John, Episode 1102, posted October 4, 2017, Desiring God, YouTube, 12 min. 41 sec., https://www.youtube.com/watch?v=ncNIuT3kIQk.

Word of God shouldn't be used in a way that is contrary to the heart of God.

If we want to combat the desire to weaponize Scripture for our own personal gain, we will submit to the Holy Spirit and His promptings. We will rely on His strength and understanding, especially when God's commands don't make sense. And when we recognize the ways in which we all attempt to misuse the Bible—whether with good intentions or bad—we will allow the Holy Spirit room to get to work.

Still Good

I know it is tempting to take a book that has been so misused and throw it out altogether, but what if we first asked the question, *What would change if we reevaluated God's Word for ourselves?* Instead of allowing other people's uses, abuses, and opinions to form our beliefs about the Bible (whether progressive or legalistic, both camps have done their own harm), what if we did the hard work and engaged in critical thinking on our own? Might there be something of deep worth and transformation waiting for us?

I spent nearly two decades allowing others to tell me what the Bible said about me, about women, about sin, about being gay, and I listened to voices that argued against the credibility of the Bible altogether. While I felt like I was treading the waters of questions and doubt, it was when I committed to looking into the Bible myself that it felt like the water started to drain and I had something to stand on again.

It was only when I became familiar with the Bible that I could, in a sense, redraw a map based on the facts I'd gathered and explore the reality around me, instead of stumbling along trying to follow someone else's secondhand opinion that misrepresented the landscape.

In fact, taking the rumors, teachings, sermons, or even hatred we have heard and holding it up to the Bible itself is a practice that was encouraged by many of the New Testament apostles.

When we look at the book of Acts and its account of the early Jesus movement, we find the story of one church in particular that was willing to ask significant questions and step into the vulnerable but good practice of eagerly searching for answers. Acts 17 states that when Paul and Silas arrived in the Greek city of Berea, they found that the Berean Jews did not simply listen to and accept whatever they were told about Jesus; instead, they were critical thinkers.

Realizing that Jesus spoke largely about keeping His Word, the Berean Jews would hold up people's teachings against the Bible to see if they matched (Acts 17:11). Was their message leading others to bear the fruit of the Spirit and grow more like Christ?

Now, I understand that to do that, you first have to find the Bible trustworthy, but what if we put the Bible itself to the test? What if instead of running to every other source we can, we pick up the book and search. Why? Because if what the Bible says is true, it will prove itself.

And I see God championing that exploration. He is not bothered or hurt or disappointed when we curiously question His Word. In fact, in 1 Thessalonians 5:21, followers of Jesus were explicitly told to test all things. God encourages our testing.

I'd like to share with you a bit of the testing I have done. Maybe you will find that we have had similar questions. Or maybe mine will spark new ones for you and give you a curious place from which to start.

Is the Bible Reliable?

Growing up around Portland, Oregon, meant being inundated with atheist arguments against faith and religion on a weekly basis. While I never cared for apologetics or arguing, I did constantly find myself curious to hear more. This brought on a bit of "bad Christian" guilt for peeking at the supposed cracks in the Christian foundation, but I eventually recognized that my God-given curiosity stirred a healthy motivation to know why I believed what I believed. From the claims that the God of the Bible was archaic and misogynistic to broader ideas of the Bible being poorly translated, I had a lot of questions—and I got to chase all of them during my college years.

Through many books, classes, and lectures, I started to notice some consistent facts about the Bible we read today. One is that we have more than six thousand Greek New Testament manuscripts and an additional nineteen thousand ancient manuscripts of the New Testament in Latin, Syriac, Coptic, and other languages—which easily refutes the claim that the Bible we have now is the result of a bad game of telephone.[4]

Some critics have said that the differences between all those translations and manuscripts make the Bible unreliable. But Chris Bruno, a professor of New Testament and Greek at Bethlehem College and Seminary, explained that, between the

---

4. Bryan Windle, "The Earliest New Testament Manuscripts," Bible Archaeology Report, February 15, 2019, https://biblearchaeologyreport.com/2019/02/15/the-earliest-new-testament-manuscripts/.

six thousand early Greek manuscripts we have today, the differences between them add up to *less than 1 percent* of meaningful variants. Even more significant, none of those variants contradict Christian doctrine, the beliefs that build our foundations of faith—such as Jesus being sinless and dying on a cross, humans being created in the image of God, all humans being sinful and in need of Christ, and the list goes on.[5] These facts also apply to many of the Hebrew Old Testament scrolls, proving that our current English translations are compiled from thoroughly reliable ancient texts.

If you do the research for yourself, I believe you'll find that people over the centuries have gone to extreme lengths to preserve the biblical text. And when you do, you might ask the same questions I did: *Why* have hundreds of thousands of people devoted their lives to copying, translating, excavating, researching, and studying this one specific book? Might it be that the contents are something of the greatest worth and value?

Is the Bible Alive?

At the end of 2022, I was sitting in a room full of pastors, preachers, and speakers in Northeast Portland when Dr. Charlie Dates, pastor of Progressive Baptist Church in Chicago, took the stage. During his talk he said something I will never forget: "I believe that the Word of God is so fresh and relevant for us today that it is newer than tomorrow's newspaper."

The room erupted in agreement with this statement, and while I sincerely concur, I also cannot help but wonder

5. Chris Bruno, "5 Myths About the Bible," Core Christianity, January 8, 2020, https://corechristianity.com/resources/articles/5-myths-about-the-bible.

occasionally what it really means. We're talking about such an old book with such ancient scribes here. I can grasp that all three of the members of the Trinity are alive today, but I still wrestle with the meaning of Hebrews 4:12: "The Word of God is alive and active. Sharper than any double-edged sword, it penetrates even to dividing soul and spirit, joints and marrow; it judges the thoughts and attitudes of the heart."

The Word of God isn't static but is operational, powerful, and living—unlike any other book that exists in this world. It is a tool that precisely separates "soul and spirit, joints and marrow." Like a butcher's knife, it can cut through our flesh, remove the rot that sin has created, and guide us on to a path toward becoming more like Christ.

Not only that, but the Bible gives us a freedom that sets us apart from the rest of the world. Instead of having to discern or judge ourselves and others, we get to allow the Word of God to do that. It will never be about us finding the inner strength to pull ourselves up by our own bootstraps; it is simply about laying ourselves down at the feet of Christ and His Word.

It has been hard for me to believe this in certain seasons, but it does not strike me as odd that those seasons have also been ones in which I have not been regularly (daily) submitting my free will to the instruction of God found within the biblical text.

During the seasons when I have committed myself to being in the Word daily, I've received the benefits of knowing the Word of the Lord. My anxiety lessened, the fruits of the Spirit were more evident, and I listened to others better. The Holy Spirit felt louder and, even in the moments when I lacked discernment, I could recall what the Bible said because it was fresh in my mind.

Many Small Books or One Big Story?

While the Word of God works to change us, it is only by one person and for one purpose. But for a long time, I would have argued that only the New Testament makes this clear. And the Old Testament? Well, that's just some good material for children's programs, with a God who needs to eat a Snickers. We could just cut the entire Old Testament—except for creation and the fall of mankind in Genesis and some lovely, comforting psalms—and replace it with a paraphrase of how terrible humanity continued to be until Jesus was born, right?

Does the Old Testament really matter to those who confess that Christianity is all about the life, death, and resurrection of Christ?

Try telling eighteen-year-old Brenna, who grew up in church, that the story of Abraham and Isaac is about Jesus, and she would have laughed and thought, *We must be reading different books.* I had grown up in churches that primarily taught the New Testament and did not highlight the continual foreshadowing of Christ woven throughout the Old Testament.

Let me tell you about one such story.

In Genesis 22:13–18, Abraham brought his son, Isaac, up a mountain to sacrifice him in obedience to God. Before Abraham did it, though, God stopped him; this was, in truth, a test of character. They needed another sacrifice to take Isaac's place, and Abraham looked up to see a ram stuck in a thicket, caught in some thorns.

God provided this other sacrifice.

Then, turning from hints of foreshadowing to explicitly naming it, an angel spoke to Abraham about Christ becoming the blessing from Abraham's children, a gift to all the nations on earth.

Chase the genealogy with a magnifying glass and follow the story, and the Old Testament goes from an ancient book to a three-dimensional map complete with flashing lights and arrows that all point toward one person: Jesus, the Savior of the world.

That is why we can be a people changed by a book. It's the story of a real person, a real God who died and rose and is alive today. Who sent His Spirit to be with us, who enables our hearts to be judged and changed by the text that illuminates our hearts and minds on the holy Trinity. A God who did not care to leave us stumbling in the dark, but desires that we come to know Him and His will, which is given to us.

By this, we can start to understand the ways in which the Bible truly is *good* for humanity. It informs and encourages; it convicts and commands; it comforts and sifts. The same book will challenge you in your weakness and give voice to your lament. It will offend and it will bring joy. And all of what the living Word does, it does in total and absolute truth.

I imagine it is not easy to fully believe that at this moment. For all the hurt and harm you might have experienced under the banner of "God's Word," I can guess that for you this brick is a big one—an odd shape that seems unimaginable to place. While some bricks I have carried Christ has put to use quickly, my experience with Him redeeming His Word has felt like waves eroding away a stone. Slow, but ever steady.

My encouragement to you is that God can use whatever pace you set. Untangling a mile of damage is just that—untangling a mile, no matter how fast or slow. So go, seek, ask, push, wonder, question, search, and do so with a critical brain and a prayer:

Make Yourself and Your truth known to me. Some days will feel like bounding down a hillside, and others will feel like weeks of backpacking. Just keep taking one step after another, fast or slow, in the direction of God's heart. That's what matters.

And where am I now? I finally understand my mom's commitment to Jesus through the spiritual practice of being daily in the Word. For it is something that has never returned void. It catches my breath day in and day out. And I am convinced that there never will be a day when there is not something new to be astounded by within the pages of God's Word.

CHAPTER 8

WOULD ANYTHING CHANGE IF I FELL IN LOVE WITH YOU?

My eyes fluttered open and shut for what I thought was every few minutes but turned out to be just about once every hour. The sterile smell, bright lights, and beeping machines were somewhat familiar, but the feeling in the pit of my stomach was not. Every time I opened my eyes, someone new was in the room. This time it was my best friend, Becca. We had met in adulthood and quickly became close.

Now, I was twenty-seven years old, and I was once again in the hospital, partly because of my own choices and partly because of my struggles.

I wasn't sure what to say, so I said nothing and instead tried my best to give Becca a reassuring smile, but as I did I could see she had tears in her eyes. As if I'd been hit by a semitruck full of emotions, everything spilled out of me. I felt horrible. My body, my soul, my brain, my stomach . . . everything ached. In an attempt to break through my confusion of being high as a kite, Becca grabbed my face to let me know she was there.

"It's going to be okay, Brenna."

Shame took over me. I kept my eyes shut. Then I cried silently until I fell back asleep.

I don't know how long Becca stayed, but I will never forget that she pressed her head against mine for what felt like an eternity and left me with one sentence that hasn't left my mind since.

"You are precious."

I had experienced rough-ish waves before, and I'd known full-on tsunamis. But in that season I'd hit a bottom I didn't know existed. And as I lay there, staring up at the light so far above me, I wondered, *Do You still like me, God?* I was squinting to try to get a glimpse of whether He was even still there. In my mind, He had other things to do. Not in a neglectful way, but just in a "You made this choice, and you can sort out your consequences" kind of way.

Of course, there was the shame and guilt that came along with hitting rock bottom. I taught the Bible, I worked with youth in ministry, I was *writing this book*. Oftentimes I haven't felt qualified because of imposter syndrome, but if you knew what I was doing in May 2023, you might literally say I was unqualified. And for good reason.

"How Do You Really Feel?"

Part of the irony here involves my complicated feelings about love. I both love it and hate it. Ask anyone who knows me well.

When someone offers it to me as a gift, I often scrunch up my nose as I try to receive it with gratitude. Hearing "I love you" often induces a lump in my throat, then an awkward reply of "I know" or a faint "love you too"—it's slightly mumbled without direct eye contact. As if a bug has landed on my skin, I try to shoo off the moment as quickly as possible.

Why? Because I hate love.

I hate the overly mushy and emotional moments at women's conferences and in churches that take place under the supposed response to "God's love." I cringe when people cry on stage (even though I do it myself all the time). I get uneasy when people say, "God loves you so much!" assuming that I ought to have some sort of emotional attachment to God.

Being uncomfortable with love has left me wondering if that aspect of a relationship with Him is actually *necessary*. Isn't it enough to know and believe? Or must we feel too?

We can talk about this more later, but now I should probably also confess . . . that I love love.

I love when Austin brings home my favorite flowers on a mundane Tuesday. When Becca hears me out when I am too intense for even myself to understand. When my mom brings me a random gift because it has a skull on it. When my dad fixes something I never asked him to fix. When Rudy randomly declares with an impressive amount of volume, "I love you, Mom!" When Rory lays his head on my shoulder in the most chaotic of moments. When my friend Lindsey checks to make sure I got a hug at some point during our time together. When my mentor, Lauren, brings me gluten-free chocolate chip pumpkin muffins "just because."

When your people know you and go out of their way to make

you feel known—that is a profound act of love. And without fail, things like this make me giddy beyond words.

I will pretend not to enjoy it too much. I will do all I can to appear aloof. But on the inside, my heart is bursting into flames of joy.

Why? Because I *love* love.

I can guess that if you are anything like me, you might struggle here too. With the way that you and I have experienced church and faith, love is the last thing we want to add in terms of the emotions and feelings being felt in this vicinity. And yet, love is talked about in numerous places by Christ Himself. All my life I have thought that knowing and understanding God was the primary requirement to being one of His followers. Now I see that living that way might be cutting us off from something significantly formational.

Before we get into the ways love could shape us, we might want to do some untangling of how the broken world has misinformed our view of love.

Origin Stories

When I was growing up, my dad and I had one hobby that we both truly loved, and even to this day, it has contributed greatly to my sense of self, fashion, and tattoo choices. As often as I could convince him, my dad and I would spend a Saturday afternoon at the local motorcycle shop. Black leather, eagle patches, and loud engines made me feel alive. I loved the smell of rubber and oil, and I begged my dad to buy a bike for me—until I started to understand the concept of money. Even so, I dreamed about us having our own bikes and going to Hells Canyon together one day.

And then came the year I turned ten.

That year shook my naively formed theology in more ways than one. That year of my life was like being hit on the back of my head with a folding chair.

My parents would argue, like most adults in relationships. Some weeks felt intense, while other weeks felt oddly okay. But as my mom's mom progressed closer and closer toward death with her cancer diagnosis, my parents seemed to fight less. My grandma passed away in August, and in October we kids were greeted with the gut-wrenching, "Can you all come downstairs? We have something to tell you." All three of us sat on the couch, my parents across from us, looking strange. I can't remember how they delivered the news, but it felt fast, like ripping off a Band-Aid.

"Your dad is going to move out of the house. He made some choices that require us to be separated for a while."

Tears, confusion, anger, grief. My newly ten-year-old brain had maxed its capacity, and it felt like it was too much. Why would my dad leave us? Why would he make a choice that would take himself away from us? Why couldn't they work it out? Where would he live? How often would I see him? How would my mom be able to manage three homeschooled kids, a full-time job, and a fracturing marriage after the loss of her own parent?

Not long after Dad moved out, I attended the basketball practice where I was molested.

You might be able to gather now what I was starting to think about "God's affection" in this season of life. My Nana was never healed, despite her faith. My dad had to leave us, and then I was molested. Three great griefs in four short months. That was all it took for me to develop a new theology of "the Father's love."

I understood that weak faith resulted in unanswered prayers. I understood that my earthly father wouldn't stick around, and my heavenly Father wouldn't protect me.

So I became a rock. Hard, cold, rough, but protected by myself—the only one I could trust. I didn't want to be known; that was only opening myself up to be hurt more. I didn't want to be seen; that would leave me vulnerable. And I didn't want to extend the love I had felt previously, either, for I believed it would fade or crumble—that I would disappoint others just as I had been disappointed. To pass on that exposure of fallen love felt unkind.

Consequently, I developed my aloof exterior, personified by a dead-eyed, tattoo-covered, stone-cold future me who resisted love.

I didn't need anyone.

Can you relate? Have you endured harm that has since closed you off or maybe made you assume the worst about God? That has made you self-protect and shut down any possibility of relating to God in the way you most longed to?

The Father Heart of God

When I was at YWAM, I kept hearing a saying that grated on me: "Just let God sing over you!" I knew YWAM was charismatic, and even though this person was referencing Scripture (Zephaniah 3:17), this stuff was *weird*.

Jesus wasn't my boyfriend; Jesus wasn't in a boy band. Jesus and I were on "head nod" terms when we saw each other, not "bask in the Father's love" terms. Honestly, I am cringing now just thinking about it.

CAN I SAY THAT?

My Mars Hill Church (a church with some crazy harmful history and a gigantically public meltdown, complete with
its own docu-podcast) era had left me with a hard heart. The
teaching wasn't all bad; in fact, I still hold some of that theology and knowledge today. But that particular "Portland, Oregon,
Calvinist" (a specific sect of Christianity that can lean hard on
knowledge and ditch almost all emotion) experience fed me a
Jesus who drank a beer with the buddies and perhaps shed a tear
or two on the cross, but never a God who held His children in
His arms. And this Jesus, this distant Father God, fit into my
childhood theology. Sure, I had come to some sense of knowing
He was for me and sovereign and probably real, but the love He
showed was about as tender as Martin Luther nailing that list of
theses to the door.

At eighteen years old, I knew and "loved" a God of tough
love. The God who sings over you, the Father who so loved His
creation to the point of giving up His own Son—that was just not
the way I experienced Him.

In those days my experience dictated the truth, but today
I cannot write this without feeling some sense of aching and
sadness. To know that I lived, and even still now live, without
a completely clear understanding of God's love for us (and our
love for Him in return) grieves me. Although we won't hold or
fathom that full understanding of His love until we are face-
to-face with Him, we can start to repair this specific brick
and use it as a cornerstone by the grace of the Holy Spirit and
God's Word.

Maybe you rolled your eyes at the last sentence. (Honestly, it
is a wonder my eyes haven't gotten stuck from all the eye-rolling
I have done in these strange conversations.) Your suspicion or

apathy is welcomed! Truly. That makes you a friend after my own heart.

Just promise me that you will read a little further, and I'll promise you I won't BS anything. I promised you and Christ honesty. I believe He will do the rest. Will you join me in seeing if that is true?

The Girl in the Pink Dress

"Brenna, I got a picture of you in a leather jacket riding a motorcycle."

My eyes lit up. People getting pictures or words from the Holy Spirit has become a normal part of my life now, but when I first joined YWAM I was new to the practice. I couldn't believe my leader had gotten a picture of me the way that I have always seen myself. Finally, the Holy Spirit was acknowledging the cool kid I had become! Until . . .

"And I just feel like the Lord wants you to be in a pink dress, dancing around freely with the Father like a little girl."

Oh, no. That is not *the Holy Spirit. That is some odd, sexist, styleless, patriarchal vision made up in the mind of someone who does not like how cool and aloof I am.* At least that was my immediate thought, and the thought that stuck with me for nine years. I genuinely love black leather and motorcycles, so the notion that God wouldn't accept this non-sinful enjoyment in my life was totally off-kilter. And how dare this person suggest God would rather see me in *a pink dress*? The one thing I have *never* owned and never *wanted* to own. I was angry that someone would think the Holy Spirit would encourage such a personal yet shallow change in someone's life.

But now, as much as I still hate the picture, I look back and think maybe I was getting stuck on the literal description when the purpose had more to do with the metaphor of it all. Yes, I am admitting that this person *might* have *actually* heard from the Holy Spirit.

I have often wrestled with and questioned whether being loved by God truly matters or not. But if God loves humanity enough to save us, and if He loves us individually enough to create and delight in us, then what are we—the tattooed, level-headed, theology-loving, apathetic-toward-affection people—to do with God's love? Can we understand love theologically but reject it in the day to day? Or are we missing out on something profound in the simple practice of accepting God's delight in His creation?

My life would suggest yes, we are missing something profound.

When I realized this, that girl in the pink dress started to make sense. My hard exterior was doing its job of protecting my heart, but now it was impeding my ability to give or receive. The problem was that I now *knew* God. I knew my heart was safe with Him. I knew I was called to love others well, and I knew receiving love, both from others and from the Father, was all a part of His good intentions for humanity. It wasn't that I was young and traumatized anymore or that I was an angry theologian either. These truths about God, the way He made me and the healing work He had done, all cleared a path for what I am still wrestling with: falling in love and being loved.

Can you also recognize this?

Being safe gives you room to experience love, and being made holy allows us to experience a new, godly kind of love.

There still is a piece of me that wished it didn't. I would *love* to stay aloof. To be totally chill. A sunglasses-on-all-the-time type of Christian. But what a waste of unexpressed and unaccepted love that would be. I do not believe Christ died so we could be tearless Protestants who don't hug goodbye or confess to anything more than stoic emotions. I believe if we begin to accept God's love, it will change us.

And as we change, God might use us for something beyond ourselves.

A Change of Heart

As people began to believe in and spread the news about Jesus across the ancient Mediterranean, the very first communities of the Christian church began to form. Gathering in homes scattered throughout cities and towns, early believers soon encountered difficulties and experienced persecution for their beliefs. Despised by Romans and hated by Jews, Christians endured pressure from all sides of their surrounding cultures. Some Jewish leaders even took it upon themselves to try and squash this good news right in its tracks by murdering those who proclaimed it. One of the most notorious leaders being a young man named Saul (Acts 8).

Until he met Jesus . . . and within a moment, his heart began to melt.

Saul, being convicted of his past life and the death and resurrection of Jesus, began to preach to anyone who would listen. As his walk with Jesus continued, the loving-kindness of the Lord deeply changed him. He would spend the rest of his life devoted to churches and people of God in discipleship.

Jailed and tortured multiple times for sharing Jesus, Saul (who is known as the apostle Paul) would spend his free time writing to his beloved communities, some of whom he had spent years with and some of whom he only knew from word of mouth. Becoming a living example, Paul penned letters of admonishment, empathy, joy, contentedness, and encouragement from a place where many of us would find torment.

In what world do you go from killing people out of hatred to enduring torture and spending your free time in prison checking in on and praying over those same people you used to hate with such vitriol? The world where we allow God's love to change us. The world where we acknowledge where there is something within our daily lives that needs to be shifted—not just learned or known but embodied.

I would argue that Paul coming to know the love of Christ was the catalyst for every other choice Paul made in his ministry moving forward. The way he taught, the way he suffered, even the way he died was informed by a deep knowing and experiencing of love from the Trinity.

You Never Did Waste Your Love

So, what things in our lives would change if we, too, lived out of a place informed by Christ's deep love for us?

I will never forget coming home from YWAM to my very non-charismatic church. I had just spent six months watching people minister to one another during every single worship session we ever had. (It's crazy to think about congregants in a church not only receiving, but also ministering to each other. Reminds me of the Bible.) Now I was in a context that never really talked about the Holy Spirit, let alone leaned into the non-pastor-centric gifts. If you weren't a worship leader, preacher, or teacher, then Sunday was a consumer experience. You would come, sit, not say anything out loud other than singing during worship or laughing at a pastor's joke, maybe greet the people around you, and then peace out until the following week.

We were in the middle of a sermon when something told me to look down the aisle to the right. As soon as I did, I knew God had something to say to this girl. She sat there happily listening to the sermon while my ears turned red and I internally argued with the Holy Spirit.

"You don't understand. This is not what they do here!"—as if that would make the Holy Spirit change His mind.

And then I heard it. Felt it. Experienced it: conviction.

Brenna, I love her. She needs to hear that. Really hear that. You have the opportunity. Will you obey?

Never in my life have I ever wanted to tell someone, "Hey . . . uh . . . Jesus loves you, LOL." I can't imagine a more awkward and cringey encounter. She was going to think I was crazy. But as I sat there, I started to remember what it was like when I began to realize God was truly and deeply tenderhearted toward me. More than the wedding vows with nervous voices or the first time you call someone your best friend. More than holding close the heartbroken sibling or feeling euphoric for the first time. More than laughing loudly late into the night with someone who doesn't care what you look like in the moment. More than the person who picks up the 3:00 a.m. phone call. More than the moment they place that tiny little human in your arms for the first time. He loves us more than all the sum experiences of love we could recall in this lifetime. And although we cannot fathom it, the small, fractured realizations of what we can fathom are earth-shattering.

That memory jolted my bones and muscles to begin sliding down across the empty chairs that separated me from this girl. I tried to look as normal as possible. I think at first she thought I was leaning in to comment on the contents of the sermon, but we would both be surprised by what came out of my mouth. I remember saying something like, "I feel as if the Holy Spirit has some specific things to say, but of course I do not always hear the Holy Spirit right. I could be wrong. Dead wrong. And I cannot over-suggest that you pray about what I am about to say and make sure it lines up with the Bible . . ." Then I whispered, and the Holy Spirit gave me words I wasn't even thinking of. I just kept sharing until the words were no longer there.

Maybe she would think I was insane. Maybe she would never talk to me again, but if I could try in my humanity to obey God well and love someone well through my actions, it would not be a waste.

As I continued nervously staring at the floor, some time went by until I heard her clearing her throat. As I looked up to accept my awkward fate, I was met with tears. I had no idea what she was going through or what she was feeling. I wasn't sure what lies she was maybe believing or wrestling with; I just knew that the Holy Spirit showed up and told her the truth: she is loved.

"You really do love her, don't You?" I mumbled in amazement that the Holy Spirit really does use us sometimes.

And you, Brenna.

That stopped me in my tracks. I didn't like that. I knew I needed to hear that, but I did not want to. That sentence and reminder continued to come up through the years, and I would try to shrug it off as quickly as possible.

"Yeah, yeah, I know," was my typical reply. But it must have been the growing experience of motherhood that started to break down my heart. And then one day I prayed another dangerous prayer.

> *Lord, I do not like this love thing. But I want to show my love for others, and I think . . . I think that would require me being able to actually sit with Your love. So would You let me know Your love? Whatever it takes?*

I don't know if I would still say the "whatever it takes" part now, if I am being honest, because it has taken a lot. A lot of things I would not choose, and a lot of things I would have never, ever, ever expected to happen. But I would be a fool not to share the Father's love I have come to know through miracles and through companionship within pain. The love that has surprised, comforted, and sustained me. The love that has most often shown up through God's own creation.

Some feel God's love through breathtaking backpacking trips or live music. It might be the stars on a summer night or an incredible single-origin, medium-roast cup of black coffee. But for me, it is almost always people.

Becca

Becca is one example of this. Never in my nearly thirty years of life did I think I needed to hear the words "you are precious," especially not from my grounded, fierce, get crap done, lionhearted friend. But I have held that moment so close to my chest every day since, because I have never known a moment that has felt more like being recognized by the Father God when I was in the very pit of despair.

Being held by the hands of someone who meant so much to me just hours after attempting to take my own life did something disruptive to me. It shook me awake. It whispered in my ears, "You are *still* known and *still* loved, and you *are* precious."

It was in those hours and days of despair, believing death was the best outcome, that I realized what I needed then *was* love. No well-written theological statement or expressed doctrine could communicate the truth I needed to receive in those days. I needed Becca, embodying Christ, to press her head against mine and declare that the one who *is* love was *there with me* in that hospital room.

And it was while walking through that season that I came to realize what falling in love with Christ could do to my battered and bruised soul. It could make me feel at home, in the arms of Christ, even at the gates of hell.

God Himself

Confessing this story to you here is a deeply vulnerable thing for me to do, even now, after I've spent years asking hard questions in public spaces. Maybe you are wondering what a grown woman and ministry leader is doing writing about doubt and suffering after she tried to take her own life. Or maybe you have a similar confession you are holding close to your chest and fear some of the same reactions. Why be honest?

Because where else would we go?

For me, I have come to know that only God has the words of eternal life. It does not matter if I would never get asked to speak again or if people view me differently. It does not matter if my struggles end up being used against me or if the stigma makes people leery of me. Why? Because Love Himself has made it safe to struggle in the light.

I cannot claim to have hope but not share how it has been there in the darkest moments for me.

I cannot claim to know peace but not explain how it has crashed into the wilderness while I was in great distress.

I cannot write about the love of God and leave out the moment I pushed myself the furthest away from Him I could ever be.

And how, even then, His love showed up.

What about you, my friend? You might still doubt that He will show up, and that is okay. Keep wrestling. Whether you delight in God's singing over you or you roll your eyes at that very sentence, there is a God who is jealous for you. He chases after those who are prodigals and those who stayed home and felt unseen. He leaves the ninety-nine for the one who would never even consider themself worthy *or* in need (Matthew 18:10–14).

There is a God whose thoughts about you are more than the grains of sand that cover this earth or the stars in the galaxies that seem to go on and on and on (Psalm 139). The God who literally dwells in eternity (Isaiah 57:15). The God who fills up *forever*. Do you get how insane that is?! He is madly and deeply in love with *you*.

We are not meant to relate to God only through *doing*—by confessing and praying and knowing His Word. He has more for us. He desires our affection because it fosters intimacy with

Him and keeps us close to His heart, and because it gives way to bone-deep change. From hatred to loving-kindness. From killing to experiencing new life. His love transforms us in a way nothing else ever could.

What would change in your life if you fell in love with Him?

PART 3

ARE YOU REALLY GOD WITH US?

CHAPTER 9

WHY DOESN'T THE CHURCH LOOK LIKE YOU?

A pastor who was smuggling drugs, a pastor who was running a cult, and multiple pastors who had affairs— these are but a few snapshots from my family's experiences spent in Christian community over the years.

If you grew up in church, you probably heard stories of moral failure or maybe even experienced them firsthand. Over time you might have grown a pessimistic view of what it means to attempt to have a holy community made up of broken people.

Maybe, like me, you have wondered, *Can't it just be me and God? Does this community stuff actually matter if the body continues to fail and sin, to cause deep pain and paint a poor picture of Jesus?*

Perhaps you have stepped away from community altogether. Church could be a place that has caused you PTSD and years of therapy, and the thought of ever going back might feel scary, because the hurt done to you has caused so much grief.

You need to know that whatever you feel, God feels it too—even more than you do. He is heartbroken at any pain caused under the banner of His name. He grieves over your suffering. He is broken with you.

Whatever your story, I hope you'll linger in this conversation with me as we sit with a question I have repeatedly wrestled with, and maybe you have too.

Why doesn't the church look like You, Jesus?

Oh, it's complicated.

And these are some of the gnarliest bricks we can collect. How could such heaps of rubble ever serve a sound structure?

Surprise, You're a Pastor

After coming home from YWAM, I knew eluding the call to ministry would be an act of disobedience to God, but I was not convinced the church was the place for me. An on-ramp to it, however, was available to me: my old youth group needed a worship leader, and I wanted a place to serve. So I stepped in as a volunteer with a low commitment level.

Volunteering soon turned into interning, and interning led to teaching, and that opened a door I never thought I would be asked to walk through.

One day as I was working at my barista job, I thought, *I've got to get a different job, one that makes more in tips.*

Then I heard with the strangest sense of clarity, *What I have next for you, you could never imagine.*

The very next day I was in a volunteer teaching meeting at Legacy Park Church when Jon, my former youth pastor and current community pastor, popped his head in and asked if I could stop by his office after the meeting.

Immediately I started wondering what I'd done that would be getting me in trouble. Had I said something too anti-Calvinist on Twitter/X? Posted too many rap songs on Instagram? Nothing I could think of would merit real intervention, but still my heart pounded a little harder than normal as I walked toward his corner office. And what he told me there stunned me.

I think the voice I had heard was the Holy Spirit; I never could have imagined the outcome of that meeting. One of our campuses was in need of an interim youth director, and my name had come up more than once. Our church had had a few women pastors in the past whom I greatly admired. I could be on that list. I went through the interview process with five other people and *somehow, miraculously,* I was offered the job.

It only lasted six months.

The first twinge of pain came after signing the contract. The hours and pay they were offering meant I would have to continue pouring lattes to make ends meet, but people do this all the time.

Then I was told that the numbers on the contract were wrong; it was supposed to be more hours and less pay per hour.

I ran the numbers and then I ran them again. I would be working for less than minimum wage. Twenty hours at the church, and I'd have to work at least thirty hours at the coffee shop to pay my bills. That would be fifty hours a week, not including all the non-paid hours that everyone in ministry ends up working.

After I had a long conversation with the pastors, they ended up honoring my original contract, but starting off on that note was discouraging and displacing.

It did not take long for me to recognize an exodus of other female staff. I went from being one of a few to one of one functioning in a pastoral role, sans the title. I did not have a degree at this point, so not being called "pastor" felt okay with me—until I started to ask more questions.

Previously, this church had held a distinction between "pastors" and "elders," which left room for them, theologically, to hire women as pastors who could teach on Sundays. But as time went on, the title was no longer given to women, and women were no longer teaching on Sundays.

Coming from Mars Hill, I had seen what could happen when a lead pastor could influence the minds of an entire elder board without transparency toward the congregation. So when the shift with women on staff was never publicly addressed, it left me feeling both insecure in my role as well as confused. I wish clarity would have been freely offered and I wish I had the maturity then to ask what felt unsafe.

My peace about continuing at the church was wavering when I got diagnosed as bipolar, and then, a few weeks later, I found out I was pregnant with Rudy. I also was only one month into my degree in theology and the Bible, and I knew I needed to give up something.

I never had felt settled in my role at the church, but I still ached at the thought of leaving because I loved youth. I loved the opportunity to wrestle through the hard reality of what teens were suffering *while also* pursuing a relationship with God. I loved preaching the Word. If I left this job, where else would I get to do this?

But it wasn't about what made sense. To pursue God's plan only when it made sense would be a faithless act.

Austin and I stuck around the church for one more year, hoping and praying for a shift. People on the fringes were hungry for truth, asking all sorts of questions: Does the God of the evangelical church care about racism? Abortion? Women? LGBTQ+ issues? Does this God care about rape? Diversity? Affluence?

You can only preach so many Sundays a year out of the Bible and successfully avoid hard topics, because the Bible has tumultuous narratives of real-life issues. Issues that God *cares* about. Monday through Friday I was being told by professors that to encounter Jesus was to run wildly toward Him with our arms full of our questions, doubts, and suffering. But Sunday after Sunday it felt like we were being pacified.

The Sunday I knew we had to leave, the pastor preached a sermon sharing about the frustration of having home appliances break down and the other joys of home ownership. My friends were knocking on the doors of the church asking if Christ cared about their addiction. Our brothers and sisters of color were being shot by police. And we were busy talking about broken dishwashers?

My church hurt could be argued against, I know. It ranges from shallow antics about being paid minimum wage to unhinged bitterness over just hoping the church would actually act like Christ. You might read this and think, *That's nothing to be hurt over.* Or you might read it and think, *Wow, that's it? Lucky you!*

I am well aware that others have been hurt by the church in much deeper ways than I have. Maybe just the thought of a church community stirs up overwhelming anger or shame for you, and this chapter feels unfair, because I can't sit across from you and hear your story. I get that. Again, I will say: God sees you, and His heart breaks with yours.

At this point in my life, I can say that the hurt I've felt from the church does not sum up my entire experience with the church; it's not that simple. I have been deeply encouraged and blessed and frustrated and puzzled and championed and stunned by the church. I also don't consider the hurt I've felt to be the end of my story with it; I believe Jesus calls His followers to be in a community we call *church*.

That is why I am writing this chapter and why I keep on wrestling instead of walking away. Jesus has not given up on His church, and I want to follow Him—even if I struggle, ask a million questions, and desperately need His help along the way.

Bitterness Becomes You

Ask almost anyone who knew me during my exodus from Legacy Park Church, and they would tell you I was a delight on social media.

No, that's a joke. (I was a jerk online.) I was twenty-three years old with postpartum depression, earnestly aching for the God I loved to be the same God churches introduced people to. The same God who met me in my theology classes and in the middle of the night while nursing, holding a baby in one arm and loneliness in the other.

I *knew* this God of comfort and confrontation, but did the church? Did the elders or the pastors? I was tired of seeing them only address men when they talked about porn. I was tired of hearing them talk about praying for future spouses and only quickly mentioning the call of singleness. I was tired of the global missions without community missions. I was tired of pastor-centric Sundays, of sermon series that lacked input from anyone outside of the straight white male perspective.

I learned to question all these things because I was at a university that loved the Word of God and the people of God. A biblically conservative school that upheld orthodoxy. That was the place that taught me to be restless for the cause of Christ.

It was this small portion of tension and frustration that led me to ask for the very first time: *Can I say that?* Can I voice my anger within the church? Can my friends ask their unsafe questions here, or will they be turned out to the world that claims there is no God?

While I thought pursuing a degree in theology would leave me with more answers, my questions kept coming, faster than I could articulate them. Would the church ever be a safe place to ask them (if I ever found the ability to articulate them)?

These conversations went from weekly to daily dialogues with God that felt disappointingly one-sided.

God, I know You care. I know You do. But the church and these leaders are falling silent on the things that those who feel unseen are wrestling with. How will they ever know that You care if the church won't show them that?

Until one day I stopped talking long enough to actually listen.

Brenna, you have a voice. Why don't you show them I care?

Oh. No. This was not what I had signed up for. This would require effort. Complaining took very little, while actually *doing* something—that was totally different.

But the excuses would be synonymous with disobedience at this point. I knew I was called to ministry, to preaching the Word and wrestling, and I now knew that it wouldn't be in the context of a church staff.

Austin bought me the gear required for a low-budget podcast so I couldn't have an excuse not to start it. I would embark on the journey to witness to those with difficult and taboo questions by interviewing my friends who had lived through those things and found God on the other side.

I talked with women who were addicted to porn. There were conversations about the actual difference between biblical womanhood and manhood, being gay in a non-affirming faith context, masturbation as a single person, anxiety, eating disorders, racism, being trans as a Christian—we were running full-force at the questions that lived in so many of our heads but that none of us ever asked out loud within the walls of our churches.

While the podcast began as an aggressive gesture toward my immediate community, it did not take long to start hitting charts around the world. This was something I never intended or dreamed of, but it only further affirmed my certainty: people want to know that God cares.

My online community started to grow, but my personal community was lacking. We weren't really going to church, because frankly, church kind of sucked, and the ways I wanted to be met by the church were being satisfied by this new ministry. But was that the only purpose of church? To have our hard questions answered?

About once a month my mentor, Lauren, would get the same text from me: "Do I really need to go to church?"

Perhaps there was an ounce of conviction that sat in my chest every time I so proudly posted the next podcast episode. I was doing the hard work that the church ignored (bold, I know). Every time I checked in to see what the church's current sermon series was, I would roll my eyes as far back as they could go and seethe for the next few hours. They still were avoiding the issues that God cared about.

Was this thought wrong? I don't know. But what I do know now is that the habit of continually throwing my expectations at a church that had already lost my commitment only made me bitter. And not just against them, but against most churches.

It was easy to find one or two churches online that, from afar, felt like they were doing everything right. I would hold these churches up against the backdrop of our past communities as if it were a fair comparison. But I couldn't honestly compare a church that had invested in me, that had hurt me, and that I had probably hurt others in, versus the picture-perfect digital download. The aesthetically pleasing online church would win out every single time, particularly because I was not doing life there. I was not in community, in the messy reality of imperfect humans.

Christians do an awful lot of talking about the New Testament churches and wanting to get back to that model. You know, the ones where everyone shared all they had with everyone else and took care of each other? And where the congregants were always screwing up and struggling with all sorts of sexual sin?

Wait *what*?

Seriously, check out Paul's letter to the Corinthians, and it won't take long to realize this early church was filled with people just like the ones you and I know today, struggling in the same ways we struggle now. From conception, the church has been made up of sinners.

Even so, the author of Hebrews urged Jesus followers to continue meeting, even in the wake of their guilt, so they could spur each other on, away from sin, toward Christ (Hebrews 10:19–25).

While God shares in our pain over the brokenness of broken community, His answer is not to walk away. He wants to reach and love His people through His people.

I know you might hear that and immediately want to bolt. I have been there; I get that.

But I want to gently invite you to stay with me in this conversation.

And I wonder if you might open your heart to the question, *Why would I assume God can't bring good here?*

What *Is* It About?

"Mom, did someone die?"

My four-year-old asked me this question as he climbed into bed with me, then attempted to push my tears back into my eyes.

"No, buddy. No one died." He got a half smile out of me with that, until he asked his next question.

"Did someone sin?"

It was June 2023, and a week earlier, the executive pastor of the church where I was previously on staff had resigned after admitting to sermon plagiarism for over a year. The day before that, the pastor at our current church, *our* pastor who had cared for us, resigned for covered-up adultery. Heartache felt like an understatement in this moment. Two of the biggest churches in our county were losing their spiritual leaders due to sin.

I looked at Rudy and nodded.

"Oh. It hurts Jesus when we sin, right, Mom?"

I nodded again.

Yes, it hurts Jesus and others. Sin damages relationships and fogs up our testimony to the outside world and to those who are struggling with doubt. When a pastor sins, the ripple impacts arguably more lives.

Did they ever even mean what they spoke? How could they preach with such conviction but deflect it in their own life? Will this always be the fate of every spiritual leader we have? And if so, why would God ever give the outlines we see in 1 Timothy 3 and Titus 1? To have leaders who are above reproach, empathetic, servant-hearted, and teachable, just to name a few.

If a pastor has failed, has the church also failed? Is the body right to be hurt, to be concerned, to hold suspicion against spiritual leaders moving forward? Or, in other words, do the actions of a lead pastor mar the image of that pastor's entire community?

When do we move from one community to the other? And after we have been burned too many times, what do we do then? When the music and the pews cause PTSD, when you yourself have been forsaken by those who gather, how do *you* not forsake the gathering if that really is the biblical command?

We had just spent three years jumping feetfirst into this community at Mountain Church. Was it time for us to go?

I lay in bed trying to listen for something, *anything*. While COVID paused our church search at the very first new community we visited, it did not take long for us to realize this place felt *different*. While people were selling toilet paper for a profit, this church announced they would be giving away theirs to whoever needed it. A few weeks after that, they authorized any member of the church to spend up to $100 on a person in need from COVID-related issues. For a church that has four campuses with twelve services, that could end up being *a lot* of money. But the emphasis was on the care of people.

While it became obvious to us that they loved well through action, I wondered if they would walk well through tension. If they would invite those asking, "Can I say that?" to join the gathering, or if the questioners would be pushed to the side. But within the first three years of being there, our church ended up doing multi-month series on racism, LGBTQ+ issues, and abortion. Talk about tension. Everything I thought the church could never be—the embodiment of Christ—the church was suddenly making a reality.

So now, I lay in bed wondering if all that was fake. If all of that would be undone.

And then I heard the questions: *Are you here because of the community or because of the pastor? Have you made church about one person or about the gathering of* My *people?*

It's always been easy to make surface-level judgments about churches. Whether they're too flashy or not flashy enough, not our aesthetic, not our preaching style, not our ideal group of community, not new enough, not old enough, not our favorite genre of worship, not a time easy to attend, it *is* easy to find the flaws that will keep us from entering in. We might rather go to a church with a pastor who has sold a lot of books or a worship team that has produced a lot of music, or one that has done the complete opposite. Or, if you're like me, you'd rather go to a church full of people who keep to themselves.

But when we synthesize the teachings of Paul to the early gatherings of believers, we walk away with a different emphasis on what the church is supposed to be—an assembly of ordinary individuals dedicated to a mostly invisible purpose: to grow up in the person of Christ and tell others about Him. Or, as our church says, to make more and better disciples. That's it.

Church was never meant to be a gathering of pastor fans or a mob of hurt people operating out of that hurt. Our churches were never meant to be *just* preaching and worship, nor were they ever meant to be *just* a meal and conversation together.

To become better disciples of Christ, we must partake in the practices Paul described. That starts with community, with togetherness. It wouldn't be enough for me to spend a weekend alone and call that church. I needed the tension and warmth of other souls to do life with.

When I stepped into that community, my weekend experience of "virtual" church changed. All of a sudden I had entered into conversations that challenged me and sparked growth. I had opportunities not only to *hear* the Word of God be taught but to *walk out* in real life what I had been learning. Confession wasn't just a weepy, overly emotional ritual done at youth camp; it was a practice that brought real change through accountability.

Church was never meant to be one dude on a stage teaching or one group of friends gathering but never really growing. For church to actually be the house of God, we must embrace both.

I have fallen into the habit of making church about "church hurt" and the damage that pastoral failures have caused. But I do think my church hurt prompted me to focus on the platformed person over the community of people. Have you been there too? How often do our eyes get locked on a system that was never even part of the blueprint of church?

Different Downfalls, Different Realities

I have been at three churches in my adult life, and none have survived without pastoral failure. Considering I haven't hit thirty years old yet, that score stings a bit.

I believe Mars Hill fell apart because it was a church built around Mark Driscoll, the cussing pastor known for his unapologetic rage behind the pulpit. Some thought it was good, some thought it was bad, but no matter what people thought, most of the "thoughts" were Mark-centered. People went because of Mark. It was famous because of Mark.

But following the news about our current church's pastor, I noticed something strange. The ache that came with the fall of Mars Hill was similar to the ache of realizing our previous church wasn't where we could stay. I held my breath, waiting for that sadly familiar ache to creep back in with our current church—but it never came. Sure, a sense of disappointment and frustration was there, but so was an odd and subtle peace. The truth was: we hadn't just spent three years of pastor-centric Sunday mornings at Mountain Church.

After not too many months of awkwardly attending "online," Austin got a text from a worship pastor asking if we would be interested in joining a community group with his family and a handful of others. That eventually turned into three years of Wednesday nights together in different friends' living rooms, multiple Sundays a year on the same worship team, and a real sense of biblical community. Although the sermons held great depth and the programs were led with excellence, that is not what kept us coming back and leaning in. It was belonging to a body that strived to become like Christ and follow the New Testament example of life together as believers.

Here we were with the brokenness of failed leadership but *also* an experience of holistic church gathering for the very first time. And that changed things.

If we left our church, we weren't just exchanging once-a-week teachings from one voice to another. We would be choosing to walk away from invested relationships that had already proved the practice to us as beneficial and *good*.

These were the people who we ate with and had good conversations with, but also who showed up. In the hospital waiting room. In the anxiety over our unborn. In the throes of job loss and medical complications. In the depression and anger. In the new seasons with sage wisdom, and in the overwhelming seasons with coffee. In the sin with rebuke and challenge, in the sickness with the laying on of hands. If we left, it wouldn't be leaving a "brand" or a building or a pastoral team. It would be leaving the sound of voices whose laughs and cries had become familiar, comforting even.

So, was the pastoral failure of one person worth forsaking the entire community?

This argument cannot be prescriptive. The circumstances will shift and the nuance will be different from experience to experience. Leaving our old church was a conviction, and staying at our current church is just as much of a conviction.

The Western idea of "the church" has and will continue to fail God's vision. Church is not a spotlight for gifted speakers and well-dressed worship leaders. Nor is it the progressive hangout session of "being spiritual together." Sure, eating a meal together is valued and necessary, but we cannot neglect being taught the Word or worshiping together. The house of God is a living and breathing organism made up of us, not a large building with livestream capabilities.

What might happen if we sought out the holistic picture of the house of God? If we stopped making it about a pastor but still valued good orthodox teaching? If we actually *regularly* practiced confession and chose to sing out loud instead of folding our arms and waiting for worship to be over?

What might change if we made an effort to make it to church every weekend and gather in smaller communities weekly? If we told the truth when someone asked, "How are you?" and actually tithed as if we believed all we have is from God Himself? If we saw gathering as a celebration of communal grief *and* joy?

What could happen if we remembered not every sermon has to be for *us* because there are other people in the room? If we let people freely express their own ways of worshiping? If we acknowledged the workings of the Holy Spirit? If we took communion and fasting and prayer seriously?

I believe it would change the way we experience God, the way we understand church, and the way the world views us. I believe *church* would become a word that means *community* rather than an institution or a building. I believe we would better embody the fruit of the Spirit. I believe, while pastoral failure would still happen this side of heaven, our communities wouldn't be hinged on their leaders' successes or failures. I believe our responses to moral failure would look more like Christ's.

Because this is what I have seen: A people who have been deeply generous and exceedingly joyful. A people who have admonished and called out for the way of repentance. A people who walk in grace. A people who value a good meal and exhort their church bodies in the ways of the Lord.

Church hurt exists. But it does not negate God's plan to have His people gather. There is a beauty in following God's lead to meet together, even in the ups and downs and brokenness of relationship.

May you seek God's face in the anguish, whether it has already come or will in the future. May you hold wisdom and faithfulness in the pursuit of being a child in the house of God. It is not a sin to weigh and to wrestle with whether the house is right in the eyes of God.

And if you have left the house and not yet come back, know that He is waiting to run out and greet you in the road.

CHAPTER 10

IF YOU CONQUERED DEATH, WHY IS IT CRUSHING ME?

Everyone always asks you what your favorite Bible verse is, but no one ever asks you which one you hate the most. I hate Psalm 23. You know the one. "The Lord is my shepherd. I shall not want."

You know what it is to *want*. You know the feeling of empty hands grasping at something that hasn't yet come and wondering if it ever will. The job, the acceptance letter, the words from someone you love, the apology, the security. For the entirety of my life, whenever I would hear Psalm 23, I couldn't help but feel significantly unseen. How could a God who claimed to know everything about me insist that there is nothing I lack? The sentiment became increasingly worse when I found the translation that worded it "the LORD is my shepherd, I shall not want" (ESV).

I would sit there pondering the psalmist's motivation. *Are they looking at me, insisting that if I have wants I am somehow stepping into sin and discontentment?* If that was the case, consider me sinful and discontent for life. I wanted a lot of things—and not just shallow things. I wanted love, I wanted peace, I wanted happiness, but life happened and my wanting continued. And every time I'd hear about the Lord being my shepherd, I'd wonder if the belief could be realized before I met Jesus face-to-face.

Can Christians honestly embody the reality of pain that coexists in the presence of hope?

These bricks feel like sand. Like something completely deteriorated in the bottom of the bag, the dust chokes us. With fear of it irritating the eyes of someone else close to us, we don't dare pull it out, even just to look at it. We keep agony tucked away, fearing exposure or the response to the exposure from our surrounding faith communities.

How Long, O Lord?

Between my broken body fighting my eating disorder, my changing mind about faith, and the daily revelations on the person of Christ through the Word of God, emotions ran high during my time at YWAM. Every day felt like a marathon, and leaning into the change was exhilarating and exhausting. I cried . . . a lot. I wanted to be healed; I believe in healing. I wanted to hear God's voice; I believe He speaks to us. I wanted to not just hear or know the Word; I wanted to hold it close to my heart and understand it, like you would a friend.

I also wanted to leave the country.

You see, part of the Discipleship Training School in YWAM usually includes three months of overseas discipleship to others. So when I found out I would be heading to southeastern China, I began to dream, and I began to want. I could hardly sit with the privilege it would be to testify about the living God I now knew to those living in darkness. I would muse about leading worship for house churches and praying with believers who clung to Christ despite overwhelming political opposition. I wanted to see revival and healing and a deep sense of joy overwhelm the people of God. I began to dream, and I began to want. Until that came to a screeching halt.

One day a leader approached me with tension in her face, then she asked a horrible question we all dread: "Can we talk?"

My stomach, filled with food for the first time in forever, churned.

My overall experience with YWAM has always felt like a mixed bag, as it was filled with life-changing encounters with the Trinity as well as iffy spiritual practices and theology. I often felt confused and misunderstood.

By now the pattern had emerged, and I knew what kind of conversation this would be. I had already sat through some one-on-ones where concerns were raised strictly by the "prompting of the Holy Spirit." Without any concrete examples of what I could change, focus on, or fix, I would leave these meetings more frustrated than when I entered them. When pushing back, I was met with, "That's just what I feel like God is saying . . . "

Today, I would know to respond: "Well, He hasn't told me that!" But I was eighteen then, and new to the practice of hearing God's voice. It didn't feel right that God would tell someone something about me that He didn't also let me in on, but I was trying my best to also respect leadership.

I braced myself for another meeting like the prior, except this one was worse.

"I don't know if you will be able to go to China. We need to see how you continue to do in regard to your eating disorder. It just doesn't feel clear."

By this point I had been a month clean from the destructive habits that came with bulimia. I had felt a huge sense of accomplishment by the power of the Holy Spirit and a sense of hope for my future. And yet . . . this conversation didn't acknowledge any of that. I wasn't consulted with or talked to or checked on; I was just informed. I was open to accountability but was never given that option. People just "prayed" about how I was doing and drew "discernment" from that. So when my reality did not match with the so-called prompting of the Spirit, I felt insane.

Fighting to get the words out of my choked-up throat, I tried to advocate for myself as best I could.

"What improvements do you need to see? When will you know if I am or am not healthy enough to go? How is leadership measuring what *healthy* looks like?"

None of my questions were answered. I sat there in the grief of the unknown, but I felt a jolt of hope when I remembered my community. Surely their prayers and accountability could serve as the comfort and encouragement I needed. But as I turned to leave, the leader said one more thing.

"Oh, and Brenna, you can't tell anyone. We don't want the other students worrying about or being distracted by this."

This was isolating. This felt unjust. I was crushed.

Every single night I sat on the hardwood floors of our rain-forest home and poured my heart out to God. "Lord, if it is Your will that I would get to go and minister to people in China, would that come to pass? If it is Your will that I go back home, would you stop letting my heart dream?" I tried hard to keep the tears from falling, but every time I sat in prayer, they would show up overwhelmingly.

Sydney, my closest friend from YWAM, would plead with concern for me to be transparent. Every time this happened, the anxiety would creep back in: if I told another student, I would probably get sent home.

What do you do when you're unbelieved by your spiritual leadership and cut off from being transparent with your community? My infant faith faced not just turbulence, but annihilation. Those early mornings amid the seventeen other silhouettes in the room, some sleeping, some doing makeup, others praying, I would open the Psalms and try to center myself. Scouring the pages for a foothold of truth, time and time again I'd return to Psalm 13:

> How long, LORD? Will you forget me forever?
> How long will you hide your face from me?
> How long must I wrestle with my thoughts
> and day after day have sorrow in my heart?
> How long will my enemy triumph over me?
>
> (VV. 1–2)

I thought surely my sorrow would subside with time, but I never found that to be true. Time was marching on, and no one could tell me "how I was doing" or what the percentage of possibility was that I would be able to go to China with my team. As we ramped up our preparations, compiling teachings and plans for VBS, I had to pretend everything was okay. It was December and my team would be leaving in fourteen days, with or without me. By now, the second my eyes opened in the mornings, the words also hit my lips: "How long, oh Lord?"

The Western world of Christianity has never lamented well. While we can turn to our Bibles and find almost half of the Psalms focusing on lament, our own worship culture reflects only a fraction of that.[1] We do not sing songs of lament on Sunday mornings, nor do we give people time to do it. Perhaps, like me, you are a product of a lamentless culture. One that has shaped us into mask-wearing mourners, never daring to let the pain of the "not yet" impact the expected joy of the "now." That is, we are not sure how to hold our aches while also holding the truth of a risen Christ, so we bury the aches. We dare not contribute to the questioning surrounding a good God and suffering. So instead we become stoic, soldiering on.

Not "Either-Or"

Monday morning worship would take place in our tiny YWAM house living room, instantly filled with heat from cramming forty-plus bodies into such a small place. Unlike Fridays at the church where you could move around, sit, stand, ask someone to go to the back if you had a prophetic word or wanted to pray for them, Mondays were like living in a fishbowl. If someone was praying for you, everyone saw. And if you were experiencing any kind of emotion . . . everyone saw. During most worship sessions I did my best to reel in the response that worship brought me to, but with the mounting *want* my soul was experiencing, this Monday was different.

I stood in the back up against the sliding glass doors, arms

1. Soong-Chan Rah, "The American Church's Absence of Lament," *Sojourners*, October 24, 2013, https://sojo.net/articles/12-years-slave/american-churchs -absence-lament.

crossed as if they could help keep in the desolation. The worship lyrics flashed up across the mounted TV in the corner of the room, but every time I tried to sing, I'd get caught up by the lump in my throat. The TV became blurry as the tears started to pool, and with frustration and embarrassment I confronted myself internally: *You're either going to be heartbroken, or you're going to worship, but you can't do both.* Logically, you are either mourning or you are dancing, but you can't do both at the same time. You're either believing God for the miracle or you are grieving your reality, but you aren't embodying both. That would be impossible, right?

Why not? Why can't you do both? Like getting the wind knocked out of me, I was caught completely off guard by a voice of kind disruption. Startled by the stark contrast in tone, I opened my eyes to see if someone else was speaking to me out loud, but of course, no one was even looking at me. The voice continued.

Brenna, beloved, does your brokenheartedness negate the fact that I am good? Or does My goodness negate the fact that you live in a broken world?

My Friend God, I felt, was confronting me with mercy and grace and truth and loving-kindness.

"Hi, God," I muttered, unable to keep a smile from cracking over my face and tears from crashing rapidly from my eyes.

Immediately He brought back to mind the verse I'd so passionately loathed for nineteen years of my life: "The Lord is *my* shepherd, there is nothing I lack."

I stood there with those two phrases, one in each hand— "Our brokenheartedness does not negate God's goodness" and "There is nothing I lack"—when the beautiful mystery fell into place.

What Psalm 23 and even the end of Psalm 13 so boldly

proclaim is a truth that stands in opposition to everything we know of the real world. In the midst of our brokenness and pain, we are fully provided for and fully met. Period. If I did not go to China, God would not forsake me. Maybe I'd feel crushed, maybe deeply troubled, but nowhere close to being defeated or abandoned. If I was never heard or understood or seen by the YWAM leadership, I was still heard and understood and seen by God. I would not be forgotten or shamed by my King, my Father, my *Friend*. And that morning I sang with a trembling, cracking voice, covered in tears because I finally knew my broken heart did not negate God's goodness.

When I walked through even harder misunderstandings and isolation *in* China, these truths served as a life raft. Speaking zero Mandarin, trying to find people wanting to not just talk to you in English, but talk about the gospel, proved to be exhausting. And when a rumor surfaced about me and my mental health that could have sent me home in an instant, I had to *cling* to the fact that God knew the truth and that He had a good plan for me. Oh, the rejoicing that came at the end of those six months when I graduated the program.

But before that rejoicing came to be a reality, I had already gotten a simple and yet significant gift. I was learning that I did not have to choose between being broken and hopeful. Christians can be both broken and hopeful.

Pregnant Anticipation

I always misspell the word "grief," which might seem ironic for a person so well acquainted with the term, but it often serves as a glimpse of comic relief in the midst of those overwhelmingly

170

dark days. You know the ones, where your breath is stolen right out of your lungs by pain itself. The ones where you realize . . . this grief is a new one, not familiar in any way. And no matter how hard you try to usher it back out the door, you are left sitting there watching as it plunders the depths of your own soul. Each minute is tense with disbelief: *How could this happen to me? Why is this happening to me?*

That is what marked September 2020 for us. With my first baby, I let anxiety consume every second of my first trimester. I remember telling Jon, before almost anyone else even knew Austin and I were pregnant, that I was scared of having a miscarriage.

With a kindness and calmness I desperately needed, he said, "You don't need to be scared."

So with pregnancy number two, I felt seasoned, even possibly protected from the anxiety of what could happen.

It is crazy, the dreams that flood your heart when those two faint lines show up on those plastic, store-bought tests. In a matter of minutes your entire being is interrupted by resounding, earth-shattering news of life. A life you haven't yet met but that already intimately knows who you are, because you, in many ways, are their own source of life. They hear your heartbeat long before you hear theirs. They know your voice before they've made a sound. The overwhelming beauty and wonder that fills your entire person could never be described in words. And neither could the loss of that same life.

Austin and I had "planned" this pregnancy (whatever that means) after Rudy Saint Blain, our precocious firstborn, turned two. Neither of us had any desire to stay a single-kid family, and besides, our kid who was just a baby weeks ago was now saying things like "Mom, that's disrespectful," and "Give me chocolate." (Let's face it, they're two sentences we all say.) So the dreaming actually began far before that positive pregnancy test.

Here I was, five years after that turbulent season of YWAM. That time had been all-consuming, but now it hardly entered into my thoughts. Only, now, a familiar feeling was returning, a new want. I was equipped, though—or at least I thought I was. I had come to know Christ in heartache, but I was sure I wouldn't face heartbreak like that again. I was right about that, in part.

I am inclined to be angry with myself for not embracing cautious anxiety that second time around, as if anxiety would have dampened the thunderous anguish we would soon be acquainted with. So far beyond the pain I experienced in YWAM, this brokenness felt infinitely darker and drastically heavier. Like the hands of terror, this pain tightened around my neck and gripped unrelentingly as it forced me to watch this horror unfold. At first I was just cramping more than usual, but I thought maybe this baby was different and maybe it would be okay. But that first sight of blood lunged for my hope. The Google searches were endless, the advice nurse sounded concerned but reminded me to rest and wait. *How long, oh Lord, can I rest and wait until that heartbeat pounds and floods me with relief?*

We never heard that baby's heartbeat. Somewhere among the loss of blood and loss of tears, their life also became lost to us. I couldn't understand what I thought I had learned all those years ago. The Lord was my shepherd, and there I stood in terrible want, lacking a stolen life. The life of my child who I would never know. I would never see what color eyes they had or if they had Austin's nose. I'd never hear that rushing cry that brings such precious relief the moments after they leave your womb. I'd never get to settle them in my arms, or put them to sleep. I'd never know their voice, their personality, their loves and dislikes. I would never know them. Oh, how I long to have known them.

The minutes felt like weeks and the days felt like years as I sat in the living trepidation of loss. Unable to feel anything outside of this new world of grief, the color left my skin as the weight trailed off my bones.

How could a good God provide for me in this pit of hell? The question sat tattooed on my heart as it faintly beat, ready to give up at any moment. Although I contemplated these thoughts with anger, an earnestness also existed. I *wanted* God to answer, truly. If He had an answer, if there was hope, if there was something there for me to hear or learn or know, I wanted to receive it. But I couldn't believe. My mind was stuck on the prior.

"Lord, if You would have been here, our baby would not have died."

Where have you felt this in your own life? You know—the pain "too deep for someone who loves Jesus"? The one with wailing that makes everyone around you uncomfortable but you cannot stand to care. Were you met with permission to lament? Shamed by your questioning? Slowly left alone in your tears? I know a few friends, besides myself and you, who have also experienced this.

My Friends Mary and Martha

Have you ever read John 11? To me, it is one of the most jarring accounts we have of Jesus' interactions when He was on earth.

While Jesus was out of town, two sisters realized their brother was getting sick, and sickness in that day and time could easily lead to death. Instead of panicking, Mary and Martha held on to hope because they knew the Messiah; Jesus had become a dear friend to their family. In their view, they needed to simply let Jesus know of Lazarus's condition, and boom, Jesus would show up and heal, like He'd done so many times before. Remember, Jesus *loved* Mary, Martha, and Lazarus.

But the next sentence flies in the face of that.

"When [Jesus] heard that Lazarus was sick, he stayed where he was two more days" (John 11:6).

Sorry, what?

Imagine this happening in the here and now. Your family member gets incredibly sick and is deteriorating fast, but your best friend is a medical doctor with a 100 percent success rate in patient recovery. They just happen to be out of town, but you know they love you, and with death in the mix, surely they would be on the next plane home.

You call them but they don't answer. You leave a calm voice-mail, believing you'll hear back soon, convinced that they've seen the message and are arranging travel plans.

More time goes by, and you send more check-in texts.

Nothing.

You call again, leave another message. Send more texts. By now your confidence is waning, and as the hours go by, your family member is only getting worse.

This is where Mary and Martha were.

And before long, Lazarus died.

Still out of town, sovereign Jesus knew this and told His disciples, "Lazarus is dead, and for your sake I am glad I was not there, so that you may believe. But let us go to him" (vv. 14–15).

For whatever reason, Christ decided *now* would be a good

CAN I SAY THAT?

time to visit His beloved friends—even though the window for healing had closed.

As He entered the town, Jesus saw a familiar face, full of grief.

Martha came up to him with an accusation: "Lord . . . if you had been here, my brother would not have died" (v. 21).

It's hard to know the hope of Jesus without also scrutinizing the questions surrounding His sovereignty. I know this. What Martha dared to say out loud many of us have screamed in our hearts.

Lord, if You had been here, my parents would still be married.

Lord, if You had been here, addiction wouldn't have stolen my life.

Lord, if You had been here, I wouldn't have been abused.

Lord, if You had been here, they would have loved me.

Lord, if You had been here, he would still be alive.

Lord, if You would have been here, everything would be different.

We acknowledge that life *with* God impacts our reality, but we still wonder why healing isn't always His plan when He is called "good." How could a God who allows suffering be good?

Maybe by now you understand why I call Mary and Martha "my friends," for they knew what it was to hear Jesus' voice and still experience life-wrecking grief.

They knew what it was like to have a confident hope that meets a wave it cannot shoulder.

They knew what it was like to tell Christ, in the face of their reality, "You messed up. This isn't how it was supposed to be."

They knew what it was like to wonder if all the things they had heard about the Messiah were true, or if they'd deeply misunderstood what "good news of great joy" could possibly mean if it wasn't on their own terms.

If Jesus showing up late wasn't disorienting enough, read what He did next.

He wept (v. 35).

In what world does this make sense? Jesus, who was fully God and fully man, had the ability by the power of the Spirit to come and heal His sick friend, but for some reason He chose not to.

And then, in the mess of grief that He could have prevented, He went in, knowing He would raise Lazarus from the dead, and allowed Martha and Mary to think He was just alluding to the coming resurrection (John 11:23–27).

Okay, that's fine. Weird that He wouldn't let them in on what He was about to do, but fine.

What really gets me is the detail that *Jesus wept.* Jesus, who could have prevented the death, who knew He was about to raise Lazarus from the dead, stopped on the way to the grave and mourned a life that wouldn't be dead for long. *Why?*

My entire life is littered with *why.* Why was I molested? Why did they walk away from their faith? Why can't my friend have more children? Why did they hurt the people around them? Why won't God heal my brain? Why can't they apologize? Why does longing feel like it's stuck deep inside my bones? Why do I still wrestle with same-sex attraction? Why did You save someone else and not them? Why did I lose this baby?

And why, Jesus, would You take time to weep over Lazarus's death when You knew what would happen next? When You could have prevented the sorrow in the first place?

Might it be that our God is not a God of quick fixes or one who ignores our humanity?

CAN I SAY THAT?

Emmanuel

As I lay on the couch drenched in tears for the eighth day in a row, I wondered where Christ was. Hollowed out into the empty space only a demolition of grief could leave, I ached. Empty of hope, empty of being known, empty of meaning—all the reminder of an empty womb. Distraction seemed to be the only thing that helped.

I'd lie there in a pair of gray jammies (a gift from a friend who had been through the same thing) with a giant pad in my underwear and watch streaming episodes on repeat. Every once in a while, for a split second, I would forget. A laugh would leap out of my chest or a smile would stretch my face and I would feel normal again. But then, as the show would go on or as we'd put Rudy to bed, the ache would come back up like the tide faithfully returning.

Again I would wonder, *Where is Christ?*

That night I got in bed before Austin. Dreading the silence, I grabbed my phone and played a familiar playlist. Barely three seconds into each song, I would hit the skip button as fast as possible. I didn't want to hear songs about God's faithfulness or goodness, not because I didn't believe those things, but because I couldn't *feel* them. I couldn't sit with the dissonance of the idea of a good God who had allowed this to happen. I couldn't worship because I was heartbroken, and because I couldn't worship, I felt God wasn't near. After all, why would He want to draw near to those who couldn't even utter His praise for the grief stuck in their throats?

My eyes scanned the title of each song and my thumbs continued swiping away the irrelevant lyrics until I saw a title that caught me off guard: "Death in Reverse" by John Mark McMillan. I knew the artist but had never listened to the song. However, with a title like that I had to listen at least once. I turned the volume up, put my phone down, and closed my eyes. I heard an acknowledgment that grief is real, that we can't control our lives, but that God is sovereign over it all.

Like a flood or the great swell of a symphony, the emotions burst out of my body. Through the chorus, there I was. Lazarus in the grave. Christ weeping. And me wondering why.

Only now, I knew.

Jesus, the man of sorrows, not only desires to give us resurrection life but also to sit with us in our suffering.

A Savior who swoops in, saves you from tragedy, and swoops back out is nothing more than a modern-day superhero. A Savior who acknowledges your pain and weeps with you in the in-between, before our eternity with Him where, as J.R.R. Tolkien wrote, "everything sad [will] come untrue,"[2] is an Emmanuel, a God *with* us.

We live in the now and the not yet, where victory over sin and death has been won. But we still exist in a broken world where sin, pain, and suffering exist, where death plunders and sickness steals and the Enemy destroys.

Yet, as Jesus sat with Mary and Martha and wept over their dead brother, He was, in a sense, saying, "Brokenness still exists. But I sit with you *in* your brokenness."

Jesus doesn't usher us quickly into the next season. He doesn't write a condolence note to avoid the tension in the room.

2. J.R.R. Tolkien, *The Lord of the Rings* (New York: Houghton Mifflin, 1954), 951–52.

He doesn't even allow the knowledge of the coming to affect the emotions of the now. He weeps with us.

I wasn't wondering where Christ was anymore, because this song had led me to Him. Christ was there, with me, mourning our baby. I also was no longer convinced that being a Christian meant hiding the pain while displaying the hope. If we are called to follow Christ, we can weep as He wept, in full knowledge of the death and resurrection.

Now, three years later, we have two healthy boys. Rory, who we got pregnant with just a few months after our loss, is now twenty months old. When I look at him, I am reminded of the God who sits with us but also of the questions that remain this side of eternity. If we hadn't lost our May baby, we wouldn't know Rory. And in all earnestness, that's not a trade I could say is or isn't worth the pain.

The truth is, with loss and with gain in its place, I still don't understand. Every time I've contemplated our miscarriage, I've been left with more questions than answers. *What type of theology allows for the loss of life before a child even lives here on earth?* I think this over and over again. Yet, I'm met with peace. A new peace in this new pain—because peace doesn't negate pain or questions or grief. Peace Himself sits with me; He meets me in the hardest parts of my pain, just like He met Martha on the road.

He greatly desires to do the same for you.

We can come to Jesus with our pain, saying, "Lord, if You would have been here . . ." and He will meet us with His tears.

He also greatly desires us to do this with one another.

We do not have to fake joy and hope in our "new life" with Christ. We can vulnerably share our affliction and sorrow, meet others' grief with our own cries, and make room for unfiltered lament and questions. If we are not honest and open, how else will the Man of Sorrows meet with us in our suffering? How else will Peace Himself sit with our loved ones in their pain? This is how we remind each other of the One who meets us with His tears.

And then later, maybe soon, maybe far off, He will meet us again with His resurrection life. I'll hold that baby like Martha held her brother, and you will hold someone dear to you too. This is the heart and will of our Father: to restore, to reconcile, to make all things new.

It is only a matter of time.

Come quickly, Lord Jesus.

CHAPTER 11

DO YOU GIVE A CRAP ABOUT MY CRAP?

It's Monday, and I have yelled at my kids more times than I'd like to admit.

I spent a great weekend with my best friends, but a lack of texts from them is making me second-guess how they feel.

I've planned dinner but never ended up making anything—so I guess it's leftovers again.

Nothing about life right now is particularly difficult or particularly amazing. And it is days like today when I tend to get in my car, drive off, and realize—there in the tiny rearview mirror—that I left Jesus at home. (If I even realize it at all.)

This isn't an "old story" from ten years ago. This literally is today. Brenna Blain, who teaches the Bible and works in ministry, forgets about Jesus.

It's probably true of most people who love God, if we are being honest. But why? And how? How could we forget the God

181

of the universe and Creator of all? The one who set us here and is literally sustaining our lives as we speak?

The God who truly saved me from suicide and loved me enough to, you know, die for me (and you) occasionally slips my mind. When I say it out loud, I sound like a maniac. But consider the circumstances.

You and I have talked about some heavy questions and difficult realities over our time together. Time and time again we have recognized the need for God in tragedy and the recognition of His intervention in miracles. The highest of highs and the lowest of lows involve our suffering Savior in obvious ways. He is showing up to weep or showing up to rescue, but either way we make a space for Him in expectancy.

But what about the in-between? Does God care about our mundane moments, days, and seasons? Can there be meaning in the times that feel kind of meaningless? These are the bricks we forget about, the ones we set aside "for later" but never come back to. The danger of this is that the pile grows and grows, and before long, we find ourselves with full bags on our backs all over again.

Full and Forgetful

We are not the only generation of God-followers to suffer from Holy Person Amnesia. Remember our friends the Israelites? The ones who, not figuratively, saw God split the Red Sea, drop manna from heaven, defeat armies twice their size, and level an entire city to the ground? The biblical authors had no problem whatsoever reporting that they also forgot about God from time to time.

"They forgot the LORD their God, who had rescued them from all their enemies surrounding them" (Judges 8:34 NLT).

"They did not remember his power—the day he redeemed them from the oppressor" (Psalm 78:42).

"They think the dreams they tell one another will make my people forget my name, just as their ancestors forgot my name through Baal worship" (Jeremiah 23:27).

Pretty crazy, huh? And those are just a few of the mentions.

So what is going on here? Are all these old writers just showing us that we're in good company when we forget God?

No. Not at all. *A creation forgetting its Creator has implications.*

But before we get there, we might want to ask why a group of people who physically, emotionally, and spiritually witnessed the God of the universe move on their behalf also let Him slip their mind sometimes. If we can answer that, we might be able to use it as a litmus test for ourselves, and I have a few theories.

Several months after the Israelites first experienced the miracle meal of manna, they forgot God. Moses went up a mountain to meet with God, and after a while, the Israelites told Aaron they were concerned that Moses had been taking too long to return. Their concern, however, did not have to do with Moses himself, but rather with wanting someone or something to worship. Moses' brother Aaron responded by giving them what they wanted: an idol, a golden calf made out of melted-down jewelry (Exodus 32).

Can you imagine a sojourner wandering up to the Israelite camp while they all were sitting around worshiping a cow—made of old earrings—then asking where he could buy flour, water, and honey to make food for himself?

Maybe the Israelites would reply, "Oh, uh, God just sends us food every morning."

"You mean the cow god?" the sojourner would ask.

"*No.*"

"No?!"

Maybe some would realize in that instant; maybe some wouldn't.

The point is, once the daily need for food was met, it was easy for the Israelites to forget God. Once their hungry bodies were satisfied, the Holy slipped their mind. Even after all that He'd done for them.

We do this too.

When we are sitting in the wake of our met needs, not yet in a season of obvious desperation, we tend to become passive.

Christianity thrives on the pendulum swing of experience. We often talk about the ways God has shown up in miracles and the way He has comforted us in a great loss. But what about when life is neither of those things? Might we be allowing these in-between times to lead us into unrecognized disobedience and a life of less?

It can be so easy for me to forget Christ's words about abiding in Him (John 15:4–11), especially when I'm standing between the peaks and valleys. It is not natural to reach beyond myself when I feel like I have enough. Or when I sense culture normalizing my less glaring sins—the passive remarks, mind-less consumption, and micro-behaviors that scream, *I am my own authority!*

Maybe you can relate.

What would it look like for us to give this flat land over to Jesus? It'd be messy and deeply concentrated work. I imagine the Holy Spirit wearing rubber gloves and a hazmat suit as we invite Him into our daily chaos. But in those places, where the *need* doesn't seem to be present, we can actually solidify our dependence on Christ.

"Remain in me, as I also remain in you," Jesus told His disciples. "No branch can bear fruit by itself; it must remain in the vine. Neither can you bear fruit unless you remain in me" (John 15:4).

Jesus was reminding His followers that they could not do this life alone, and the same is true for you and me. Not only is God the life source of all that we are, He also is the source of our fruit: the love, joy, peace, forbearance, kindness, goodness, faithfulness, gentleness, and self-control that turn up in our life is only a result of knowing and being in him (Galatians 5:22–23). Each of these fruits turns us away from the "micro-sins" that compile into habitual monsters.

"Do not forget Me," Jesus was saying.

"Keep depending on Me, day after day—whether you're in a valley, on a peak, or on flat land."

"I am your source, always."

When Creation Forgets

In 2020, sometime after the pandemic had shut everything down, I was in the thick of what felt like a new normal in my ministry. After having all my speaking engagements canceled, I approached God with a sense of questioning. Was I really discerning that this was what He was calling me to if there were no longer opportunities to walk in that calling? Or was this just some grand scheme of my mind?

After some waiting, I felt as if the Holy Spirit were reminding me of the small group of followers I had collected on social media. What if I could offer something of worth, pointing back to all that God has done on there? Maybe I could be an encouragement to at least one person, and it would continue to exercise this teaching gift when I couldn't speak to live audiences.

Nine months later, my following on social media had more than quadrupled, I was getting asked to do multiple podcast interviews a month, and in-person speaking invitations were coming back into consideration.

The day I cracked ten thousand followers on Instagram—a coveted achievement, because it unlocked premium features at the time—I was elated, floating even. But in the next moment, the feeling vanished. It wasn't enough of a dopamine hit for me; I wanted more.

A quick Google search to a sketchy website offered a great deal—one hundred "real-looking" Instagram followers for five dollars. It wasn't enough to sit at 10k. I had to have the security of 10.1k, even if it wasn't real.

What had started off as an earnest pursuit—to bear witness to the hard yet real ways Christ penetrates our brokenness and offers Himself—somehow turned into idol worship. How?

That season of life became a blessing, and then it became normal, and then it became wildly mundane. It felt easy to write about God and theology, and uneventful to have conversations surrounding the implications of sexuality and faith; life seemed monotonous.

I also fell into the lie that just because I was talking *about* God, it was basically the same as talking *to* God. But it wasn't. I wasn't seeking God, because life was typical, unvarying, and almost stale. I wasn't listening for His voice or consistently reading His Word or worshiping. As I was coasting in the mundane and typical, there was a rotation in the throne room of my heart; God was ushered out and Instagram was ushered in.

I was just like the Israelites, when their stomachs weren't growling but their minds were continuing to itch for someone—or rather some*thing*—to sit in that place of honor. I forgot God, just like they did.

When life is easy, we, the creation, forget the Creator. And when creation forgets their Creator, we replace Him with idols. I think that because we were made by someone beyond our-selves, we have the constant need to have someone or something lord over us, something beyond us that we look to for truth or comfort or to be pacified, seen, valued, heard, met, loved, fed, sheltered . . . the list goes on and on.

We can find this idolatry in the media, our friends or family, and certainly ourselves. It might be work, a partner or spouse, money, ministry, control, friends, being known, art, collecting knowledge, consumption, drugs, exercise, sex, good grades, fashion, excelling, escaping, writing, or pursuing perfection. All these things have been idols for me at one point or another. But none of them could bring me life.

You Don't Remember, Do You?

When I first started speaking, I would type up a short list of bullet points to carry to the pulpit with me. (Well, it wasn't really a pulpit because we were nondenominational, so it was just a tall table.) Inevitably, I would get to the end of my sermon, leave the stage, and then realize in horror that I had forgotten a major point with great theological implications or that something I had said came across as unclear (at best), leading the listeners to confusion. Not what you want in a Bible teacher.

So, the next time I would get asked to speak, I would practice more beforehand. I would put more effort into the repetition, thinking that this would solve my problems.

While it helped, it was never foolproof. The nerves would show up with blinders. Time and time again, I would listen back over the recording and think, *How can this keep happening?! Why can't I remember?*

Interestingly, this was a reflection of my personal life at the time, in one of the most easygoing seasons I have ever lived through. I was working as a barista—in the Pacific Northwest, this is a sought-after job—and interning at my church. My boyfriend and best friends led worship with me every week, I was speaking every couple of months, and I was traveling the world a few weeks at a time.

But between slinging coffee, leading small groups, and visiting Scotland and Frankfurt, I would find myself wondering, *Does anything I do actually matter?*

As a Christian, the answer is obvious; we know the Author of meaning! But that doesn't mean it's not something we won't wrestle with internally, especially as we interact with the world around us.

Anxiety and apathy would creep in for me in subtle and nuanced ways. I'd drink a little too much and I'd sit in the sadness a little too long. I'd be a little bit mean—not too mean but just a little bit. Selfishness would get in the way of kindness. Melancholy would beg for permission to find meaning in anything except its actual source.

I knew and believed in the basic truths of who God was and

what that meant in relationship to me and to others, but without a daily reckoning of my soul back to Jesus, the resurrection life didn't transfix my reality. It didn't sink in deeply to the crevices of my entire being; therefore, I did not reflect what I claimed to believe.

Just like in my preaching, when the words weren't right in front of me, consistently, I could not remember the life I had been given access to.

I struggled to remember that there can be meaning in the mundane.

The unwillingness to abide in Christ in the easy season was as tragic as the kind of speaker I had become, unwilling to write my sermons in their entirety, something that I would realize I needed to do. I just kept missing the mark. I could not be bothered to implement effort in my dearest relationship, which, of course, begged the question: Was it *really* my dearest relationship?

This culminated in months of worry. When I was twenty-one years old, I was in yet another country on someone else's dime to head up a camp for Christian youth. What a dream! Except I was tipsy a decent amount of the time the nights between camp sessions. Why? Longing.

Does anything I do in life really matter? my soul kept asking. It wasn't an overwhelming feeling, but it was present enough to make me want to forget it.

Would the people who had seen me stumbling around a missionary campus on Cinco de Mayo wrestle with what my actions said versus what my mouth had proclaimed?

Even though I quit drinking soon after that trip, my question lingered. *Does anything I do in life really matter?*

Just a year later I'd find myself in that psych ward. I cannot pretend to understand the entanglement of our choices in life and the brokenness we are subjected to. But I do wonder, if I had woken up in the morning and sat with Christ and in His Word daily, would that have changed anything for me in that season? I think maybe it would have, even if it was having just an ounce more faith.

Broken Longings That Carry Us Away

When we, the creation, forget our Creator, our longings and questions become subject to wandering off, looking for the next best thing. They pull us away from our best love and life source. They lead to distraction, brokenness, and anxiety.

This can look like apathy, drunkenness, and depression.

But it can be seen in less extreme ways, too, like our disrespectful interactions at work and our shortness with family. Our crude humor with friends or mindless consumption. There is a restlessness in our souls that carries us away from the abiding life.

I can see it in my impatience with my needy young sons; I get caught in my longing for relief from the daily frustrations.

I also can see it in my tendency to feed my soul sad music and let myself sink into melancholy. While of course there is a time and place for sadness, I can overdo it and steer my heart into heaviness, preaching gloom, not truth, to my soul.

My old favorite, Psalm 13, shows me how to move from sorrow into hope, though.

> How long must I wrestle with my thoughts
> and day after day have sorrow in my heart? . . .
> Give light to my eyes, or I will sleep in death . . .

> But I trust in your unfailing love;
> my heart rejoices in your salvation.
> I will sing the LORD's praise,
> for he has been good to me. (vv. 2–3, 5–6)

We live real lives, full of the mundane and, frankly, full of crap. Everyday stressors, disappointments, or boredom can leave us with broken longings, and without exposure to truth, we can lose ourselves in those longings.

But let's not forget: our God did not rise from the dead simply to release us to live unchanged lives. Salvation is just the beginning. If you believe in the life and resurrection of Jesus, then you get to acknowledge the Holy Spirit and continued sanctification.

When Christ was talking with the twelve about abiding in Him, He knew the Holy Spirit would empower them to do so. Not long before Jesus alluded to Himself as the vine of life, He explained that the Father would send them His Spirit, the Helper and Advocate (John 14:26–27).

This is the exact same Helper and Advocate you and I have today.

The Holy Spirit illuminates the teachings of Christ, reminds us of the truth, and gives us peace. This information is often concentrated in the peak-and-valley moments but forgotten in the in-between. But that is not how we were meant to live. In the abiding of Christ and the housing of the Holy Spirit, we have an opportunity to live a life of the holy mundane, and it is radical.

How? Let me show you one example.

Consider a bad habit you once had but then managed to break. Maybe it was smoking or never doing the dishes after dinner. You resolved to make a change because of the bad effects.

Maybe you had trouble keeping up physically because it was hard to breathe. Or you would get to the end of the workweek with a mound of dishes that took time away from what was supposed to be a restful weekend.

Once you kicked the habit, you experienced relief and newness. You could play sports with your kids and hike without struggling. Or your kitchen was clean at the end of every night, which gave you a sense of peace and more free time on the weekends. Your day-to-day became significantly better because you implemented a practice to do, or not do, something.

How much more significantly could our daily lives change if the thing we implemented was not a simple new habit, but communing with the Holy Spirit?

Implementing

As we have already seen, God's people forgetting Him is not new. The Old Testament describes God's people forgetting Him not only for months at a time, but for generations. King Solomon caused his own demise by forgetting all God's commands, and almost every king after him made the same bad choices. Over time, God's people had adopted idol worship, sexual immorality, slavery, greed, and other forms of dehumanization.

If one of us had been born as the next leader in the middle of this story, it'd be easy for us to act the same way all the others did; it would have been all we'd ever known and the only history we'd ever been taught. But one king, the youngest of them all, decided to change course and turn back to God.

King Josiah soaked in Scripture, and he was overcome with how much God's people had pulled away from God and given themselves over to sin (2 Kings 22–23). He resolved to lead them back to God and submit to His Word, moving in a way deeply contrary to the kings before him.

Josiah instituted public and communal readings of God's Word for all the people to hear. He renewed the covenant of the Law with God's people. He reinstated the practice of Passover. The domino effect was the removal of false gods and idols, doing away with pagan priests and idol shrines, and radically transforming the kingdom. From top to bottom and left to right, an entire kingdom was changed because one man implemented his convictions from God and the instruction of God in his daily life.

While this may be an extreme example of how remembering God can change a kingdom, our effort to keep God at the center can be just as revolutionary.

When Creation Remembers

Have you ever met someone who just embodies peace? They stand out, don't they? In a world and culture that is set on hurry and hustle, these unanxious souls present themselves to the rest of us as an odd yet inviting oasis. We think we know the same Jesus, or rather know Him in the same way, so we have to ask what makes those people different. Most Christians profess the peace of Christ, but a much smaller percentage let Him infiltrate their lives. And when they do, it is hard to look away. They talk differently, carry themselves differently, and listen more intently. And their witness prompts questions from others and inspires change.

I know this because I know my friend Caitlyn.

Caity and I never really met; she was just always around.

She was athletic, smart, and three years older than me; we didn't really have a reason to be friends. Despite that, I will never forget the moment I realized she knew I existed. I was standing, probably somewhat awkwardly, trying my best to participate in a youth group game, when she shocked me by saying, "Brenna, come stand over here!"

Sure, she was just a student leader doing her job, but to me, seeing someone take the effort to remember and use my name instead of the normal "hey you" struck a chord with me. Come to find out, this slightly different approach to life is Caity's norm.

By now you know my somewhat reckless tendencies, especially in high school. I was dramatic and weird, and, as my senior year approached, my small-group leader stepped away from her role when she left for college. I wasn't really looking for someone else to take her place and lead me, but ever so subtly, Caity recognized a need in my life.

She practiced confession with me—*me*, of all people. She'd give me a small glance from across the room when I was about to make a questionable choice. She'd offer gentle, short words of encouragement. She just constantly showed up. Not loudly or ever begging to be "my person," but always just to make sure everything was okay, whether I saw it or not.

These micro-habits woven into the fabric of Caity's being have continued to set her apart. To this day her presence invites you to just *be*. I never have to mentally prepare for our time together, nor do I have to try and hide the reality of the current moment. She is easy to be with, yet she has conviction.

Caity knows the voice of her Father, and knowing Him beckons her to walk in step with the Holy Spirit. For years I wondered what it meant in Acts when Paul quoted the philosopher, saying, "In him we live and move and have our being" (17:28). And I now see Caity as a walking, breathing, familiar example of this.

As busy parents, Caity and I have connected most through paragraphs of texts stitched together with a coffee date every four or five months. As she considers all the mess of words and emotions and worries that tumble out of my brain, more often than not, she consults the Holy Spirit as she responds, because she believes that is how we are called to do life. She's a living temple who *knows* she's a living temple.

This isn't just apparent in the big, interpersonal communication moments but in the mundane as well.

She finds small ways to love people well. She weighs the consequences of actions before stepping into them. She is quick to return to her Father and slow to pass judgment. I have never known Caity to rush into something without waiting on the Lord. Even in her anger, she lives it differently. She wrestles; she doesn't just walk away.

All this is informed by God and through the instruction of the Word. I know Caity is great, but I also know she's not like this on her own, nor has she always been like this. Only through abiding in Christ by the Holy Spirit can she embody the freedom and peace that Christ gives.

As Caity went from being a leader to a dear friend, I got to see behind the curtain, which brought clarity to my questions about abiding in the mundane.

When creation remembers their Creator, they fight to keep Him on the throne of their hearts.

It is not that Caity or any other unanxious soul lives perfectly and free of idols, but, like King David, they relentlessly seek repentance and redemption. Through constant reexamination of their heart condition, they are made people after God's own heart.

It has taken me some time putting the pieces together to realize what makes Caity different, but now that I see that it is her simple willingness to *not stay far* from the Father, I have to ask, *Might I be missing out on something that is freely available to me? To us all?*

Making Effort in What Matters

The path into this way of life may seem kind of mysterious, but it's actually very simple. Conceptually, anyway.

It is spelled out plainly in the book of James: "Do not merely listen to the word . . . Do what it says . . . Whoever looks intently into the perfect law that gives freedom, and continues in it— not forgetting what they have heard, but doing it—they will be blessed in what they do" (1:22, 25).

It is a simple yet difficult command: *Do what it says.* Four words. That's it.

If James were here today, I am sure he would look at us and preach the exact same message. While I have been busy looking for the secret to being able to cling well to God in every situation, the book of James is holding up a giant neon sign that I instinctively would like to ignore. Because doing what the Bible says takes effort. It takes intentionality and time away from other things. It requires sacrifice. Not only do you have to make time to read the actual Bible, you also have to make time to implement what it teaches.

To break bread with fellow believers, to be generous, to be merciful, and to reconcile.

To return to the secret place, to praise wholeheartedly, to ask the Father for things earnestly.

To keep unwholesome talk from your mouth, to abstain from lust, to be sober, and to hope.

To keep the Sabbath, to confess sins, to be a faithful servant.

The list goes on and on.

Sometimes this all just seems like not a fun pill to swallow, I know. But this isn't simply a list of tasks that have become our duty; it is what it means to be made alive in Jesus and live out the life God has won for us. This is what it looks like to love Him enough to stay close to Him, to worship Him and keep becoming like Him.

Ultimately, the call on those who have placed their faith in Jesus is to be transformed, not to be preserved, not to be comfortable. And this is meant to play out in all seasons, including the ordinary, mundane ones.

There are two profound truths that can help us as we move in this direction.

First, if we are followers of Christ, we have been given the gift of the Holy Spirit, and He makes all this possible. With Him, our lives can start to look radically different. We can experience the results of His presence: love, joy, peace, forbearance, kindness, goodness, faithfulness, gentleness, and self-control (Galatians 5:22–23).

Transformation will begin when we actively invite Him to work in and examine our hearts, over and over and over. We might notice a pull to spend time with our Father. And when we spend time with Him, both through prayer and His Word, our hearts will start to align with His will. The Spirit will keep reminding us of what is good and right and true.

I can tell you from experience: this actually happens. I have found myself compelled to listen more, hope more, and offer kindness in places of tension. I have found myself striving less and finding contentedness in more situations than what I thought was possible. I have started to hear and sense the Holy Spirit more and more.

When we seek God in the mundane, the small things will become easier. And then they will add up. This is the second truth.

Learning to abide in Christ within the mundane will solidify your dependence on Him in every season of life.

Jesus once said that listening to Him and putting what He says into practice is like building a house on a solid foundation. When the storms come and the winds rail against that house, it remains intact because it has been built in such a strong way (Luke 6:46–49). He wants to build us up during every season of life, and He can do that only when we keep turning to Him and coming close.

We live in a broken world, and the peaks and valleys are inevitable. But the recklessly good news of Jesus is simply that He is enough.

When pain comes, He is enough.

When a miracle is delivered, it is because He is enough.

And when you are in the in-between, wrestling the mundane and apathy and poor attitudes, when the kids won't stop crying and you got cut off in traffic, when your barista got the order wrong and you are already running late, or when you're just wondering, *Does any of this actually have meaning?* you can know it does.

God desires to use it all, and because of that, normalcy can be a gift that anchors us to Him.

CHAPTER 12

ARE YOU WORTH IT?

People often think that the yes I gave Jesus at age nineteen was the hardest choice I've made. That placing a stake in the ground, agreeing to surrender my sexuality to Jesus, was the biggest deal.

But I want to be honest with you in our last few moments together in this place. *That* yes was easy. The yes every day since then has been harder. There has been an abundance of blessings as well. But I won't deny how intensely I struggle.

Perhaps this is why I run to the book of John over and over again, like a child running toward their favorite pair of arms. Words like these from Jesus reassure me that I am not crazy and bring me comfort: "I have told you these things, so that in me you may have peace. In this world you will have trouble. But take heart! I have overcome the world" (16:33).

He did not say *you might* have trouble, or *hopefully you will not* have trouble. It was definitive; *you will* have trouble. It is to be expected in this world.

I have lived in the land of trouble, lived amid shadows cast by doubt and torment produced by suffering. So I have saved my biggest and hardest question for last.

Is Jesus worth it?

Is Jesus worth the trouble? Worth the sacrifice? Worth the strange interactions with others? Worth denying your wants? Even the wants that feel like needs? Is it worth living with convictions that keep you from doing things the world enjoys?

Is He worth the sorrow, the denial of easy outs, the shaping of character that breaks parts of us away? Is Jesus worth the faith that is required to follow Him?

What if I cannot do it perfectly? What then?

And are words from Jesus, like "Take heart! I have overcome the world" in John 16:33, really able to change my life? Can we truly believe that He will give us unmovable hope and mountains of joy? That we will never be left alone, but that the Holy Spirit will actually show up in our weakest moments and sustain us in our times of most desperate need?

But What About . . .?

I am afraid some pastors and churches have made an entire living off of trying to tell us Jesus is worth it because of what we can gain in return. Some sly and poor interpretations of the Scriptures will have us believing that strong faith equals comfort, and if you aren't experiencing that comfort, something is wrong with your faith.

But Jesus our Comforter never meant an earthly promise of comfort.

And, again, He did promise that we would have trouble.

We see this clearly in the life of the apostle Paul (and pretty much every other apostle we have record of). When writing to the Corinthians, Paul shared his equally impressive and horrific list of troubles brought on by his *yes* to Christ: beatings, shipwrecks, stoning, being lost at sea, imprisonment, nights without sleep, and days without food (2 Corinthians 11:23–33). These are just *some* of the results of a life committed to Christ.

Can a modern preacher with health insurance and a huge house say his version of faith is stronger than Paul's simply because of his lack of suffering? I personally see that leading to the opposite conclusion. If Paul could still utter "God is good" as the crowds were closing in to stone him, might his God look more powerful, more holy, more *worth it* than a God who gave an already affluent preacher a car with a six-figure price tag?

Like I said earlier, my initial *yes* to Jesus was the easy one. It is today's yes—with the kids screaming and pulling at my legs, the frustration of trying to find *another* new medication, a marriage's honeymoon phase that has long been in the rearview mirror—that is harder. I have no desire to sugarcoat what life is like pursuing the narrow path.

It has now been three months since I overdosed, and almost every night I still wonder why this is my life, why I am mentally ill. Why my brain works against seemingly everything, including my spirit. Why I still struggle with the temptation of same-sex attraction.

As with most struggles, it comes in waves. A wide and easy path often calls my name. The one that suggests the occasional drink or illicit use of drugs would take the edge off. The one that says, *It's okay if it's just a conversation. It won't lead anywhere.* The one that says, *Linger in the attention a little bit longer. You deserve it.* The one that gives me permission to be defensive on social media, to seek small doses of pleasure, to ignore my kids and close out my husband.

At the bottom of the pit, those offerings feel like a ladder being thrown down to me. That ladder, that wide and easy path, looks enticing. It looks like rescue. It looks like a promise in a dark place, which seems to be a reoccurring accommodation for me. Forget checking in for a few nights—I think I have a lease here. The pit is not foreign to me.

I am sure you know your own pit well too.

Perhaps your pit has become a bit of a shelter from the religious zealots who have flashed their Bibles at you like weapons. Or maybe your pit houses many others whom you have formed a new community with, and you wonder if leaving the pit will mean leaving them too. I do not know what it is for you, but I do want to acknowledge there is so much to consider. Your pain, your history, your struggles, your comforts, all these things matter, and all these things hold weight. I do not want to sweep past reality. It is truly so much to consider.

But as much as I have known the land of trouble, the pit of despair, I have also known the kindness of the Lord in those places. Living with and sharing about the two, the struggle and the grace, has been wildly indescribable, but let me try to tell you what it's like.

In Between Camps and Tribes

The Westboro Baptist Church set an early impression of "God" and His people in my mind. A legalistic dictator with hot-faced followers screaming for me and others to *just change.* According to their enraged theology, the only way I could be accepted into the kingdom of God was if I could be made straight.

I imagine that you, as much as I, have not been a stranger to this wicked false gospel. But as we have gotten to know the *real* God through our questioning, we are given a much different picture. A real picture of the God who meets us in the road with tender eyes and a wide smile. The God who calls us precious while He gently presses His face to ours, the God who weeps with us, the God who is actually here in the room communing with us.

It was the real God pitted against the legalistic God who led me to ask: What other loud convictions divorced from compassion have turned people away from God? What false theologies have presented a Savior who only flips tables but never communes with sinners, when we really have One who would look past the religious crowd just to extend an invitation to a hated tax collector, our friend Levi?

As I was trying to make sense of the messages about God I received from Westboro, I was hearing competing ideas from another direction. I connected with people with similar struggles online, and while I appreciated their friendship, they consistently made attempts to rearrange my view of Scripture and Christianity overall. One friend would send me articles and YouTube videos suggesting that the verses outlining sexual immorality were translated wrong or that standards of morality had changed since they had been written.

While the Westboro Baptist approach of evangelism was outright hateful, this approach caused greater wrestling with my questions about God. Does love always mean acceptance? Does God dictate wrong and right, and if so, has He made that known?

I had accepted the idea that to live out my own desires would mean I would not be choosing the way of Jesus. But as our conversations went on, my friend kept communicating that my natural desires *did* align with the Creator of the universe (even though they did not align with Scripture).

Every single time I thought about this, that promise from the book of John came back to my mind: "I have told you these things, so that in me you may have peace. In this world you will have trouble. But take heart! I have overcome the world" (16:33).

I didn't know if I was going to end up loving Jesus, but I saw three different paths to choose from. The first had heavy burdens piled on by legalistic leaders, like the bricks we've been told to keep hidden in the bags on our backs. The second had seemingly no denial of self and no crosses to bear, claiming that following Christ isn't all that hard, because He wants what our hearts want.

The first seemed crushing and utterly contrary to the heart of God.

The second seemed to claim a version of Jesus that did not reflect His Word. Compassion ripped away from the foundation of truth leads people to a false gospel.

So what about that third path? It's the path I have found myself on, the same one, in fact, that the tax collector Levi ended up on. It's where broken people are met not with legalism or progressivism but with the Holy One.

The Third Path

When you and I first met, I told you how the passage about Levi challenged my legalistic belief that to be invited we must first get cleaned up. But I left something else out. Something that I hope is both encouraging and challenging to hear now.

Let's look at Levi's story again—and a bit more of it than we read before.

> While Jesus was having dinner at Levi's house, many tax collectors and sinners were eating with him and his disciples, for there were many who followed him. When the teachers of the law who were Pharisees saw him eating with the sinners and tax collectors, they asked his disciples: "Why does he eat with tax collectors and sinners?" On hearing this, Jesus said to them, "It is not the healthy who need a doctor, but the sick. I have not come to call the righteous, but sinners." (Mark 2:15–17)

When Jesus said that we are sick, He was implying that we are in need of Him and His Word—all of it.

His invitation to us isn't just a progressive call to hang out for a while and leave unchanged. How do we know this? Because of what happened to Levi the tax collector.

Levi witnessed the person of Jesus, who embodied compassion and upheld truth, and recognized, "I have a choice to make." To follow Jesus was to never return to that tax booth. The comfort and safety and self-satisfaction and sin that was Levi's daily life had to be abandoned if he were to follow Jesus.

When Jesus says, "Follow Me," He is not suggesting we make some simple gestures toward proximity or weekly gatherings or a public label. The invitation to follow Him is a summary of every single biblical command and truth we have been given.

Jesus does not crush us under horrific expectations, nor does He allow our fickle hearts to lead us off the narrow path, distracted by things not of His will.

His burden is easy, *and* we will have trouble.

How is that so, as we now live in a Matthew 11:28–30 and John 16:33 world? How could we ever "take heart," as Jesus says?

Because this is the only path where the literal prize at the end is the same person who walks the path with us. When we submit ourselves to the lordship of Jesus, He becomes our guide on the narrow path. While the trouble is promised, so is the ending. He has overcome. He has the victory. His Spirit is here and with us.

So what does that look like in the now and not yet?

Immeasurably More

First, it looks like contentment.

And I mean contentedness *in and out* of the trouble, not just after it's all over. Not just after you have caught your breath or cleaned yourself off.

Paul knew all about this, after all he went through. He said,

I have learned to be content whatever the circumstances. I know what it is to be in need, and I know what it is to have plenty. I have learned the secret of being content in any and every situation, whether well fed or hungry, whether living in plenty or in want. I can do all this through him who gives me strength. (Philippians 4:11–13)

The construction of Paul's confession is jarring here. In his use of the word *whether,* he implied that, even in our deepest wants and hunger, Jesus is enough.

Jesus never said that God's plan is that we would never go hungry. God's plan is that we would *experience His sufficiency* in our hunger and out of our hunger. And that gain is far better than any riches and any comfort.

Why? Because the gain is *Him*. Having Him right next to us.

Just as He wept with Mary and Martha, and with you and with me.

Just as I wrestle with the temptation of my attractions that promise me love the way I want it. Not only can He keep me from my temptations, but He can actually deliver relief and sufficient help in the midst of my needs. It's what Isaiah was describing when he wrote, "You will keep in perfect peace those whose minds are steadfast, because they trust in you" (Isaiah 26:3).

Second, it looks like peace.

God ordered my thoughts when I sat, again, alone in the psych ward.

He delivered me to a place of peace, even as I still struggle with the reality of ending up there.

He has reminded me I am more than a body when I struggle with the ache of having an imperfect one.

He has overwhelmed my scared soul when wondering if the bleeding would ever stop and the baby would live.

These all are pictures of what we read in Lamentations: "Because of the LORD's great love we are not consumed, for his compassions never fail. They are new every morning; great is your faithfulness" (3:22–23).

Third, it looks like a relentless pursuit of love out of great compassion.

No distance or anger or disbelief I could lob toward Him in my seasons of questioning and no fickleness of my heart today could dim His affection or slow His forgiveness. Even while I was knowingly sinning, He bore that sin and then still chose me.

While I have suffered as a result of my own sin as well as the sin of others, God in His goodness and redemption has taken my suffering, doubts, and questions, and allowed me to see Him and know Him more clearly through them.

God could have made me straight, but because I struggle, I get to know the power of calling on the Holy Spirit, the comfort of being seen by Christ, and the hope of one day being made whole with God.

It is through knowing loss that I have come to know the man of sorrows.

It is through grief that I have been reminded of the gift of knowing love and learned how to accept love when shame could more easily take its place.

As Austin Blain says, "Everything I think I don't have, I actually have in Christ."

I am a person changed, not yet fully healed or relieved of temptation, but changed by a compassionate God who invited me to come close.

"You are safe here," He said.

Through His compassion and my first small steps with Him on the narrow path, I started to experience a God who isn't just enough, but "who is able to do immeasurably more than all we ask or imagine, according to his power that is at work within us" (Ephesians 3:20).

As I kept bringing all my bricks—all my questions, hurts, and doubts—to lay at His feet, I finally realized His compassion was leading me to a conviction to cling to His truth, His Word. It offered me new life.

Jesus' truth offers *you* new life too.

It's not a life of lugging around bricks in shame or pretending they don't exist. It's a life that orders the chaos and takes those bricks and makes a dwelling place.

Mine is not anywhere near complete; the walls are barely chest-high. But the foundation has been laid and I know it is firm. As I look around, I find myself encouraged by those who are working on their roofs.

Some might say, "That is an awful lot of bricks she once carried," but all I see is the home Jesus faithfully built for me.

Order out of chaos.

Purpose out of pain.

A dwelling place for God and me, together, built on mercies and grace.

God is the only one who can give us these miracles.

To experience them, you have to leave the tax booth, like Levi did. But what came first for him? Sitting at a table with Jesus, sharing a meal with Him. Simply drawing near and getting to know Him, Levi ultimately came to see Jesus as someone worth trusting. Worth being vulnerable with. Worth following.

So the last question I leave you with, friend, is this: *Will you bring your bricks to God?*

This is the God who is able to do immeasurably more than all you could ask or imagine.

The God who knows your heart better than you do and desires more goodness for you than you could dream up.

The God who wants to hear your unsafe questions and hidden doubts.

The God who invites you to come close, *just as you are.*

And with eyes of compassion and love says, "You are safe here."

Will you bring those bricks to the real God?

ACKNOWLEDGMENTS

When I sat down to write this book, a sea of faces came to mind every time my fingers hit the keys. I am only here because of others, and this story only exists because of countless people's *yes* to God. I owe a great deal to a great deal of souls.

I first need to thank Kathleen Kerr and Carrie Marrs, who labored over this book as if it were their own. The way you each have empowered and encouraged me throughout this entire process has been deeply forming. I am an author because of both of you. And to the W Publishing team for taking a chance on an angsty girl with big questions and for refining the work to an even better end. You all kept me focused on the goal: Jesus.

To Mom and Dad, for laying a foundation of faith that I eventually came to recognize as good. For praying for me for the past twenty-eight years and loving me unconditionally. And to Carolyn, Jim, and all our siblings for being part of the many hands that made this light work. It is not easy to do the work-life balance, but our parents made it possible and loved our boys outrageously throughout the process.

Acknowledgments

To Lauren and Matt Bowen for relentlessly showing up time and time again, in accountability, hardship, and joy. Lauren, I love you so deeply, more than I can put into words. To Jon Siebert for seeing me, calling me a "pastor," and telling me I could teach the Bible to whoever would listen. And to Gerry Breshears for not letting me fall between the cracks, for giving of your time and wisdom, and for never failing to pray for and with me.

To Rebecca, for being there.

To those who we call our community: Chad for being our pastor in so many ways, the Leonard C. G. for being our people. To the individuals who prayed, encouraged, loved, cheered, and have held us close: Caitlyn Friesen, Lindsey Ponder, Kendra Leeanne Kuntz, Ali Gadbaugh, Jennifer Henderson, Andie Davenport, and so many more.

To Phylicia Masonheimer for first calling me a writer.

To my online community: so many of you have prayed for me and did it daily. I truly love you and feel spoiled to have you as a part of my life.

To Rudy and Rory for the gift that you are; my heart is overjoyed to be your mother. May you come to love Jesus all of your days, despite how I have imperfectly reflected Him.

To Austin. You have given me waves of encouragement, gentle admonishment, days of rest, and now, years of joy. To experience sickness and health with you has brought me to fall in love with you all over again, for I have come to love being held by you no matter the circumstances. Thank you for choosing me day after day. Thank you for only ever telling me to run after what God has put in my heart. Thank you for being meek and mild. You are so dear to me.

Acknowledgments

Finally, my Friend, Comforter, and King. Jesus, You have kept me when I could not keep myself, saved me, loved me, taught me, forgiven me, disciplined me, never forsaken me. May Your will be done on earth as it is in heaven.

ABOUT THE AUTHOR

BRENNA BLAIN is a contemporary theologian from the Pacific Northwest. While she speaks to and writes on many topics, Brenna is most passionate about God's involvement in our pain and personal struggles, including mental illness, same-sex attraction, and abuse. Connect with her on Instagram @bunonmyhead.

PODCAST

CAN I SAY THAT?

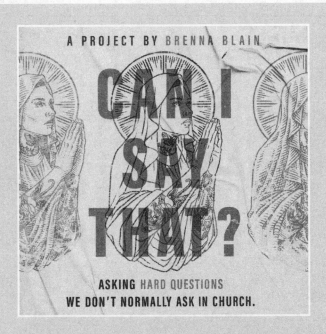

A PROJECT BY BRENNA BLAIN

CAN I
SAY
THAT?

ASKING HARD QUESTIONS
WE DON'T NORMALLY ASK IN CHURCH.

Engaging with culture as Christians in a post Christian world, asking questions we don't normally ask in church. A project by Brenna Blain.

Some topics include:

**SEXUALITY AND GENDER • MENTAL HEALTH
POLITICS • THEOLOGY**

Former guests include

**LISA BEVERE • JACKIE HILL PERRY
JOSHUA HARRIS • PRESTON SPRINKLE**

BRENNA BLAIN

Does your church need to hear about God's good plan for our sexuality? Do you run a conference that could use help speaking to the intersection of faith and suffering? Or do you have a ministry that just needs to know God cares about our deepest questions and taboo thoughts?

Brenna Blain's ministry exists to help your people understand and know the God of the Bible who is not afraid of our hard questions. You can hire her to teach or speak by going to www.BrennaBlain.com.